COSTUMES AND CHARACTERS
OF THE
British Raj

COSTUMES AND CHARACTERS

OF THE

British Raj

EVELYN BATTYE

Illustrated by
CECIL ELGEE

Introduction by
M. M. KAYE

Webb & Bower
EXETER, ENGLAND

Frontispiece:
Jakko Temple priest's assistant, Simla

Published in Great Britain 1982 by
Webb & Bower (Publishers) Limited
9 Colleton Crescent, Exeter, Devon EX2 4BY

Designed by Vic Giolitto

British Library Cataloguing in Publication Data

Battye, Evelyn
    Costumes and characters of the British Raj.
    1. India—Social life and customs
    I. Title   II. Elgee, Cecil
    954.03'5'0924   DS421
    ISBN 0-906671-42-6

Typeset in Great Britain by
MS Filmsetting Limited, Frome, Somerset

Printed and bound in Hong Kong by
Mandarin Offset International Limited

Contents

Introduction

M. M. KAYE

It seems to be customary to begin a foreword by saying 'I feel very honoured to be asked to write an introduction to this charming/interesting/informative book' . . . or words to that effect.

Well, as it happens, I wasn't asked to write this one. I offered to do it. Firstly, because Miss Cecil Elgee's delightful sketches illustrate the India of my youth—that lost India-of-the-Raj that I can still see clearly in my mind's eye, lit as though with the diamond-bright rays of sunrise on a clear morning. A land to which (if God is kind enough to allow me any choice in the matter) I shall hurry back the moment I die. Secondly, because the many types of people she drew and painted with such enthusiasm, when she herself was young, can still be seen in the free India and Pakistan of today.

I saw them all myself less than a year ago and was exhilarated to discover that despite the rash of skyscrapers and the influx of Western technology, they had not been swept away like flotsam on the roaring tide-rip of these modern times. Any traveller who cares to look can still find most of them, which is a reassuring thought and, to me, a very comforting one.

My last reason was because the text that accompanies Cecil Elgee's pictures has been written by a friend of mine: one Evelyn Désirée Battye, whose husband, Stuart, is a grandson of one of the ten 'Fighting Battyes'; three of whom—Quintin, Wigram and Fred—served in the same Indian Army regiment as my husband, the famous Corps of Guides, and died, one after another, leading their men into battle. I have written about these three in one of my novels, *The Far Pavilions*.

There is also another, though very tenuous link, between myself and the Battyes. When, back in the last century, my kinsman Sir John Kaye (who was no mean writer) died before he could finish his contemporary account of The Indian Mutiny of 1857–8, the officer selected to complete the task he had been forced to abandon was a certain Colonel Malleson. And this is the dedication he wrote for his first volume of Kaye and Malleson's *History of the Indian Mutiny*:

In the hope that this book may live, I dedicate it to the memory of my brother-in-law, Quintin Battye, of the Corps of Guides, one of the first of the many gallant men who gave their lives for their country on the Ridge before Delhi. The words which he uttered when, on the 9th of June, 1857, he received the wound which he knew to be mortal, *Dulce et Decoram Est Pro Patria Mori*, were cherished as a most precious inheritance by his brother, Wigram Battye, who, entering the service after his death, was appointed to the same regiment, the Corps of Guides, and by unflinching gallantry and devotion won from the stern frontier men who composed it the esteem and affection which they had borne to Quintin. Following throughout his noble life in the footsteps of his brother, he emulated him in the manner of his death, for he too died leading the Guides in a gallant charge against the enemies of England, at Fatehabad, near Jellalabad, the 2nd of April, 1879. Similar as was their life, similar as was their death, I would not separate in this dedication the two gallant brothers. *Par Nobile Fratum.*

Malleson had married the only sister of the ten 'Fighting Battyes'. And at the time that he wrote that typically high-flown Victorian dedication, he was not to know that fifteen years after Wigram's death, Fred too would die in the same fashion—leading the Guides into action.

After that brief digression into the past, I would like to move back again into the twentieth century and tell you a little about Cecil Elgee, and how she came to draw and paint the pictures in this book.

She has, she says, always scribbled, drawn or painted on any piece of paper that came in handy, ever since the day when she was presented with her first paintbox at the tender age of five—or possibly six? She cannot be quite sure: though she admits to a vivid recollection of that momentous event, largely because it led to the discovery that 'a little Prussian blue goes a long way'. She put this to good use by proceeding to paint her face and much of her clothing blue, and as a punishment for this venture into the realms of futuristic art, was shut into the bathroom by her mother, with instructions to wash her clothes. Here, unfortunately, she discovered a blue-bag which she added to the water. 'Result—a spanking from Dad when he came home.'

(Any readers who do not know what a blue-bag is have only to ask their grandmothers. Or better still, their great-grandmothers!)

Having left school in 1921, Cecil, with her mother and sister, set sail for Bombay, where her father was Chief Engineer of the Backbay Reclamation Scheme: a project that involved reclaiming a large tract of land from the sea by throwing out a vast containing wall. A thriving section of modern Bombay now stands on this spot. And here, oddly enough, is another tenuous link—this time between Miss Elgee and myself—because when I was sent Home to school in England, the father of one of my closest friends was Sir Lawless Hepper, who was in overall charge of the Backbay Scheme, and I can well remember his daughter Cynthia telling me about it.

Cecil Elgee's stay in India lasted for nearly six years. But though based in Bombay, from time to time she and her family visited a number of hill stations in order to escape the rigours of the hot weather. Among these was Simla, where they stayed at Mashobra, which lies some five or six miles outside Simla on the road to Tibet.

Both my sister and myself were born in Simla, and we lived out at Mashobra for several happy years, in a house on a ridge of the hills. That house still stands, and though there have been changes, the stupendous view from its verandah, windows and garden remains unaltered. Every snow-capped peak of the far ranges and every fold in the hills were, when I last saw them, as familiar to me as the lines on the palms of my hands. The only jarring note was the mule-track from Tibet that ran just behind our house, and along which the Tibetan traders and their women used to pass with their wares on their way to the shops in Simla. Any reader who is familiar with Kipling's classic, *Kim*, will know what those wares were, for the shop of the 'Healer of Pearls' was stocked with goods from Tibet, and Kipling has described them in detail. But nowadays the mule-track is silent and deserted, for China occupies the lands of the Lamas, and the frontier of Tibet is closed. But when Cecil Elgee was in Mashobra she would often have seen, as my sister and I did, the Tibetan traders plodding along the track with their panniered mules. And fortunately she was old enough, and talented enough, to be able to capture them on paper.

She too, as we were to do a decade later, travelled to the delectable valley of Kashmir where she floated in a shikara on the Dal Lake, saw the many bridges over the Jhelum River, the ancient mosque of Hazratbal (now, alas, pulled down and replaced with a large and blindingly white marble copy of some mosque near Mecca), and camped among the pines at Pahlgam. She also visited Agra and saw that wonder of the world, the Taj Mahal, and wandered round Imperial Delhi—the old Delhi of the Great Moguls. And everywhere she went her sketch book went with her and her busy pencil was seldom idle. Even at State Balls in Government Houses, she would make notes of colours and the details of uniforms on the backs of the little dance-programmes that were in vogue in those days.

From the moment she landed in India, the people and their costumes fascinated her, and she lost no time in enrolling herself as a part-time student at the Bombay School of Art. Here, apart from the headmaster (a post once held by Lockwood Kipling, father of the great Rudyard), she was the only European, and her Indian class-master gave her invaluable help, not only as a teacher, but because he could tell her so much about the different costumes, and the people who wore them.

Having only brought out her old school exercise books with her, she had to acquire the materials she needed from the Bombay Stationary Mart—a place that many 'old India-hands' will remember with nostalgic affection. Here she bought the Rowney's sketch books, sketch pads and loose-leaf sketching pads, the Winsor and Newton's sketch-boards, paints and brushes, the pencils, rubbers, mapping pens and indian ink that were the tools of her trade. And there was, of course, never any shortage of subjects. She even drew while being taken for drives in the family's 1920 Ford car; jotting down hasty notes on the scenery and the people that she passed.

The grimy carriage windows of the rattling, chattering, dusty trains that carried us all every corner of that fabulous subcontinent, provided her with endless material. As did the nerve-racking drive up to Kashmir, along those miles of winding, perilous mountain roads that separate that green and flowery paradise from the scorching plains. And it was while being driven along that road that she almost came to a sticky end when the Indian driver became delirious, owing to a sudden attack of malaria, and almost succeeded in driving the car over the edge of a precipice. Others have not been so lucky, for such accidents were by no means uncommon on the Kashmir road. I know every yard of it only too well, and it has frequently scared the daylights out of me!

Cecil Elgee says that at first she drew and painted 'largely for her own amusement', though I suspect that, like all those with an artistic bent, she could no more have stopped drawing than breathing. But inevitably there came a day when the editor of *The Bombay, Baroda and Central Indian Railway Magazine*, who, as a personal friend, had seen some of her sketches, asked her to illustrate one of the articles in the magazine, and later promoted her to staff artist. Then the GIP Railway engaged her to do black and white drawings for their magazine and brochures, and three-colour cover designs for their time-tables, and *The Illustrated Times of India* began to publish her work. The Oxford University Press employed her to illustrate school books, so as you can see she was kept busy. And happy, too: as all artists are when they are engaged in 'doing what comes naturally'—except on those exasperating occasions when nothing that one's pen, pencil or brush does will come out right!

India was and always will be a paradise for artists and writers. So much so that even people who have previously insisted that they 'couldn't even draw a line', let alone string two readable sentences together, have been known to rush out and buy a paintbox or a loose-leaf notebook, and struggle to put down on paper something of the glamour, squalor, or sheer blazing colour of what they see around them. We owe a debt to enterprising people like Cecil Elgee, who worked so hard and compulsively—and kept so many of her drawings. And to women like Evelyn Battye, whose recollections of times past have added so much to them.

Evelyn's father was a Captain in the Royal Navy who had earned a

DSO and bar. His wife died when their baby daughter was only two, and Evelyn was brought up by his American mother-in-law in the south of France. Years later, when her grandmother died, Evelyn accepted an invitation to work in India as Personal Assistant to the then British Resident in Kashmir, Sir Denholm Fraser—universally known as 'Dem'.

Since this overlapped into my own time, and my parents were great friends of the Frasers, I must have met her on more than one occasion, though I am ashamed to say that I have no recollection of having done so. Presumably because she was too busy? The job was certainly no sinecure, for PAs were expected, like Voltaire's Habbukuk, to be *capable de tout*, and most of them were. However, the work was not without its rewards, for Lady Fraser's maiden name was Battye, and she had two brothers serving in India. The younger, Stuart, was commanding a troop of Bengal Sappers and Miners, based in Risalpur, on the road to Mardan, and though Evelyn does not tell us about it, it was not long before romance blossomed between the Resident's brother-in-law and his pretty young Personal Assistant.

However, as any reader of this book will soon realize, the writer of the text that explains and accompanies Miss Elgee's pictures is describing events that she saw from a ringside seat. For example, that incident of the dish of peas that was inadvertently tilted all over the Vicereine, happened at a banquet in the Bangalore Residency ('Dem' was by then Resident in Mysore) given by the Frasers for their Excellencies the Viceroy and Vicereine of India, who were visiting the princely state of Mysore. Evelyn, among others, helped to pick peas out of Her Excellency's coiffure, tiara and the expensive folds of her dress, and dealt (competently, one is sure!) with the distracted Mr de Mello, who was responsible for the disaster.

But there is something else that Evelyn has not told you. The name of the man who saved the life of the little Raj-Kumar, Bapji—beloved only son and heir of Fateh Singh, Maharana of Udaipore—when the child lay dying from infantile paralysis and the *hakims* of the court could do nothing to help him: that man was her father-in-law, Walter Rothney Battye of the Indian Medical Service, DSO, Companion of the Order of St John, Chevalier de Légion d'Honneur, son of Richmond Battye, a brother of Quintin, Wigram and Fred, who served in The Corps of Guides.

How could I resist writing an introduction to a book full of pictures of 'mine own people'—as Kipling called them in the dedication of one of his best known collections of stories about India—and with a commentary by the wife of a grandson of one of Wigram Battye's brothers? Besides, my father's name was Cecil, and no one ever had a better father!

I wish this book every possible success.

COSTUMES AND CHARACTERS
OF THE
British Raj

Few passengers were out on the boatdecks in time to see the dawn just beginning to tinge the stark outlines of the Western Ghats. It was my first glimpse of India—a dramatic, unforgettable experience during the last years of the great British Raj.

More and more people began to crowd the rails around me as the liner slowly made her majestic way through the narrows at Kolaba Point into Bombay's vast land-bound harbour, full of British warships and merchant vessels. We craned our necks the better to see the towers and flat roofs of the Queen of Cities crimson-streaked in the growing light.

The magic of India had held generations of Britons in thrall since the seventeenth century. Now, in the years between the two world wars, I belonged to the last generation that was to come under its spell when India was all India, the whole subcontinent. What was it, I wondered, watching the unfolding panorama, that made India so special? There were other sunrises as beautiful as this; there were other countries as dramatic, as exotic. Was it India's vast diversity, from the lonely coldness of the mighty Himalayan ranges to the crowded sweat-bath of the Cape Comorin coast? Perhaps it was the contrast between the rolling pine-clad hills and the torrid desert plains, or the mixture of races, the hundreds of religions, the temples, mosques and palaces? I did not know, and when I asked one *koi-hai* (old-timer) who loved the country, he gave an evasive answer as if shy of voicing his feelings. I would have to find out for myself.

On board were seasoned British officers returning to the Indian Army after eight months' leave; the box-wallahs in their tussore silk suits— the mercantile men, bankers, businessmen and heads of famous firms, and wealthy socialites visiting India. Some would be travelling on to the Far East on P & O ships whose names began with a C, such as the *Chitral* and the *Canton*, China-bound.

Their lofty situation on the upper decks seemed peculiarly suitable for the first-class passengers, for they were known to those they ruled as the 'heaven-borns'. They were the Raj—from the Hindustani word for rule—who were 'high born': the Governors, Commissioners, Residents, Judges, all who came directly under the Viceroy, the King's representative. The Raj Ruler was the King Emperor himself, the *Kaiser-I-Hind*, and not only did he rule India, he ruled half the world as well.

These 'heaven-borns' were returning with their lady-sahibs, their *burrah* mem-sahibs, and their chaperoned daughters known as the Fishing Fleet. That particularly apt description had been applied to any unmarried female arriving in India since the steamship and the Suez Canal had reduced the discomfort and length of the windjamming months round the Cape to a cruise of a mere six-thousand-odd miles. These families partook of a leisurely breakfast in the dining saloon as the ship ghosted in to the harbour; soon they would be whisked off in private cars, leaving their staffs to deal with the mundane details of disembarkation. Some were driven to mansions along the coast, others were put up in suites at the Taj Hotel until their time of departure; others had their own white-painted rail coaches, equipped for a long journey across India, hitched to the train of their choice.

These top men were few in number, nor were there many of the more junior members of the Indian Civil Service and the Political Service—a thousand or so governing hundreds of millions. The oiled machinery of the system worked so smoothly because of the army of Indians who staffed it, a long line of men going back to the 1600s when 'John Company' (the familiar name for the Honourable East India Company) built the first trading posts with their protective forts. Without the goodwill, industry, honesty and loyal application of the Indian civil servants the British could not have governed. That was British India. The rest (and it was a large rest) were the Princely States, ruled by hereditary maharajas and rajahs, the British having a Resident, like an ambassador, in each state.

In the second-class accomodation we were mostly young, short of money and full of pleasurable anticipation. For myself I viewed the scene with mixed eagerness and apprehension. My initial excitement started to evaporate when a blast of hot air came from the shore, bringing

a whiff of drains and stinking garbage. I had been watching the tugs busily pushing and gently nudging the liner into her berth at Ballard Pier, and once she was stationary, the heat was like facing an open oven door. With sinking heart I saw the jostling, shouting mob below, and began to wonder how I would ever get through that milling crowd without becoming hopelessly lost.

A fear of being lost had been with me since the grandmother who brought me up had died and I found myself alone. Then, to change the whole course of my life, came a letter bearing a lilac-coloured two-anna stamp with King George V's crowned head on it, asking me to join the staff of one of those very heaven-borns! A subsequent letter contained a list of clothing to bring—no less than *six* evening dresses—with instructions to purchase a bedding roll at the Army & Navy Stores.

That there were dangers in India I knew, of course. I knew that it would be exceedingly hot in the hot weather, and humid and enervating on the coast. I knew I could become ill—very ill—that I could die, but then so could I in an England where as yet there were no antibiotics or sulphanilamides for pneumonia, no penicillin for infections, no serum prophylactic for poliomyelitis, nothing for diphtheria but a tracheotomy operation with a tube inserted through the throat, nothing for tuberculosis but to go to Switzerland and cough one's heart out.

In India there were added dangers. European women were more likely to die in childbirth, and child mortality was high. There were cholera, rabies, plague, typhoid, typhus, dengue and dysentery, and I would get malaria—everyone got malaria with no preventative for that either, though it was treated effectively with quinine till one was infected again and swung into the next high–low fever bout. In India of course there would be added dangers (not to mention earthquakes and floods) but even if it all ended for me out there under a dazzling white tombstone, I would have lived another life, I would have seen a whole new world.

I came down to earth with a bang in the customs house on the Bombay quayside, a long boiling-hot tin-roofed shed, which took two hours to clear in spite of the help of the Cox & King's man. Outside I was relieved to find that someone had been sent to meet me. The sun beat down on the unfamiliar white headgear I was wearing, a rather round affair known locally as a Bombay bowler and by others as a Missionary topi, a term used by snobs and nabobs who for some reason I could never comprehend wore khaki topis.

Hustled through a horde of beggars, I was horrified to see their fly-encrusted eyes and their deformities as with outstretched hands they rushed at us in a tattered throng, some propelling their truncated bodies on roughly made trollies. The crying wail came over in a chorus: 'Baksheesh, Mem-sahib, baksheesh baksheesh, *ek pisa dō,* give one *pice*!'

'*Hāt-jao hāt-jao*, go, move away there!' my escort shouted in an authoritative voice, dispersing the crowd. He told me the sheer numbers

of them made giving largesse an impractibility, and reassured me that as well as being plentiful the beggars were also professionals, that none starved, that they all had a roof over their heads, be it only a tin shanty. Bombay prided itself that few slept out on pavements in the thriving twenties and thirties.

Then we were in a bull-nosed taxi-cab, my cabin trunk tied with string on to the grid at the back, my bulky bedding roll up-ended on the seat next to the Sikh driver. It blocked my view to the front, which was just as well as he drove like Jehu, hunched over the wheel with one hand permanently honking the horn, his full pink lips smiling happily between the thick moustache and beard gathered up into his *pugri* (turban).

Taken on a short tour of the city, I was shown the huge Victoria Terminus Station looking exactly as it sounded, a vast turreted neo-Gothic Victorian edifice where all the great journeys of India started and ended, including the famed Frontier Mail to Peshawar on the North-West Frontier. At this station a patient crowd, far bigger than that on the docks, waited in tens of thousands for their trains.

From there, along the harbour front, we passed the Taj, a hotel that looked more like a palace with its five arcaded and ornate balconied storeys topped by a large central dome, lesser ones at the corners. It was said the English architect committed suicide after coming out to see how his work was progressing and found it well advanced but facing the wrong way, inwards, into a mean little road. Opposite, to the front of this favoured rendezvous of old India hands, was the Gateway of India, built to commemorate the visit of King George V and Queen Mary in

1911. The Gateway was like a wider Arc de Triomphe, the inside and surroundings kept clean by sweepers, the beggars kept out by a blue-uniformed policeman. Steps led down before it to where boats with awnings vied in offering cheap trips to see the famed cave-carvings on Elephanta Island in the harbour.

The car began to climb up green Malabar Hill and along Ridge Road to the residential area with its rocky gardens cut out of the steep cliffs. From there were far-reaching views out over the Arabian Sea of long-prowed dhows with beautiful lofty sails. These sea-going boats were swept across from Africa with the trade winds, reaching India in May with their cargoes of fruit and ivory, and bringing the monsoon to drench the country. In September and October the dhows returned with the wind, laden with cotton, tea, spices and silks.

The houses on these heights overlooking the Arabian Sea had electricity, a slowly turning punkah sited centrally overhead in each room. Only in the cities and in the official residences and Government Houses was there electricity in the twenties; in the cantonments and messes of regiments, in the bungalows, in the district magistrates' houses up-country, in the smaller towns and villages there was no electricity until the early thirties, and in remote districts it did not come till much later still.

From my recent reading of every book on India I could lay my hands on (as well as struggling to comprehend an Urdu phrase book) I knew on arrival that there had been Buddhist settlements around Bombay as far back as the third century, that Maratha raiders coming in from the sea

brought Hinduism to the settlement as shown in their cave-temples, as well as bringing terror; that the Portuguese were the first Europeans to arrive (in the sixteenth century) and develop the natural harbour of Bom Bahia. The small port was given as a dowry to Charles II on his marriage to Catherine of Braganza. The British occupied the Seven Islands, a vilely smelling swamp apart from the mainland where some fishing tribes lived. It was to become one of Asia's largest seaports, the lovely harbour with its inshore islands, bays and creeks attracting not only the British with their eye for eastern trade, but also many nearer to hand.

It attracted those from the Katiawar Peninsula, and those from the low-lying Kutch Basin to the north, the Gujaratis by Ahmedabad, the Marathas from the Deccan Plain in the Central Provinces, the Goanese from their tiny colony further south; it attracted the Parsis from as far away as Persia, and those from Northern India and many more from South India, all converging on the developing port and staying to become Bombayites. Cotton mills were built; textile industries burgeoned; factories rose from shacks on watery stilts; ships from every nation crammed the harbour—and Bombay flourished in a unique culture of its own embracing every religion and caste, a place where all India met, rich, middle-class, poor, black, brown, white and Eurasian. All these various people lived peacefully in a tolerant society under the benevolent Raj which had taken over the government of India from the East India Company in 1858.

Naturally there were grumblers, and more than grumblers, those who felt passionately that progress was too slow and who demanded home rule. They were the Nationalists (in 1885 the Indian National Congress, strangely enough, was founded by an Englishman, Allan Octavian Hume) and the Congressmen with their Gandhi caps, whose voices—led by that saint-like, skeleton-thin 'Father of the Nation'—could not be ignored by successive viceroys who advised Parliament in London. Indianization was gradually taking place in the twenties, to gather momentum in the thirties for an eventual independence few denied would come; the only question was exactly when.

This about the country and the Raj I already knew, and more I would find out as I learnt the language from a *munshi* at one rupee (7½p) a lesson, and began to travel widely—among other places to Udaipur, Jaipur, Agra and Delhi, up to Simla and as far as the North-West Frontier and Kashmir.

Wherever I travelled over the vast subcontinent that was India, I received nothing but friendly smiles and helpful hands from the colourful kindly people of the land. A woman alone on the road was as safe from rape and murder as nowhere else in the world, only vulnerable, like everyone in India, to stealthy theft. So exceptional was violence to women that shocked indignation had broken out when headline news told in 1923 how Afridi raiders in the North-West Frontier town of Kohat had murdered Mrs Ellis and kidnapped her daughter Molly, holding her to ransom. Horrified voices declared nothing like that had happened since the Mutiny nearly seventy years previously. (Subsequently Molly was rescued by Mrs Starr, a brave missionary, who journeyed in tribal dress with a party of men to the Afridis' hide-out in the bleak mountains and brought the girl down unharmed.)

Because of these rare events, and because there were some chores neither sahibs, nor mem-sahibs, nor miss-sahibs could do for themselves in India, travellers of any standing took a personal servant with them. Mine was a Pathan called Yakub Khan.

He was the one who made all the *bundobast*, the arrangements, the one who saw that the metal tray, slopping with water on the floor of the miss-sahib's compartment (Women Only), was periodically refilled with a large slab of ice; he brought me food and drink, or conducted me to the restaurant car (if there was one) at a station stop. There were no corridors on trains, and the stops for the third-class passengers to embark and disembark—many sat on the roofs or clung to the doors from the outside—were frequent.

At nights, for eventually when I went north and south, east and west, many nights were spent on the trains traversing thousands of miles, Yakub Khan undid my bedding roll on the bunk, made it up with sheets and pillow case, and all but tucked me in. He looked after my welfare with deferential politeness, but never slavishly. Underneath his manner

I was left feeling that he didn't think much of me: he was only doing this out of duty to the Resident sahib, my 'high-born' boss.

It was not long before I began to perceive that the fierce black eyes which sometimes glinted scornfully at my ignorance—as when I asked him if those people spitting out blood on the platforms were ill with tuberculosis and he told me the red was the betel-nut they chewed—could also be humorous. *Hoh*! nothing better than a joke at the miss-sahib's expense.

This was brought home to me on my first night on a train when I found myself alone after a wealthy Parsi lady had departed with all her many packages. After making up my bedding roll Yakub Khan carefully put up and locked the outer wooden-barred shutters and the inner wire mosquito-proof one. Then this hawk-nosed man from the Frontier warned me of thuggee: 'Plenty thugs come along train roof with sharp *khangar* in hand,' he explained graphically. 'They dacoits, *budmarshes*; they climb in and steal.' As if this warning was not salutary enough he added as an afterthought, looking at me blandly, '*Budmarshes* watch out for Miss-sahibs travelling alone!'

Of course I slept not a wink after that, expecting at any moment to see a shadowy figure forcing its way through the window intent on slitting my throat. Next morning with a sigh of relief I opened the shutters to see Yakub Khan (having himself slept well in the corner seat of the crowded servants' carriage) being shaved by a *nai* (barber) on the plat-form, after which with his pugri back in position on his close-cut grizzled hair, he brought me a mug of hot tea. Then, rolling up my tossed bed, he shook his head mournfully, exclaiming, 'Miss-sahib not sleep well? *Hoh* . . . Miss-sahib was afraid!'

I laughed. What could one do but laugh with them? They were such marvellous contrasts of faithfulness and fickleness, of loyalty and roguishness. They were at times incredibly hardworking, at others utterly indolent. They lived together in large family units with little privacy and no loneliness, the very old and the very young helping in the fields and in the household chores as much as their ages allowed. They were generous, the poor giving to those even poorer, they were resilient in adversity, and they were wise with wisdom that had nothing to do with education.

I was beginning to understand. *They* were the magic. The lure of India lay in its people—in their mass each was an individual, each a character.

Kolis, Bombay Fisher-folk

Within easy walking distance of the Gateway of India, through the colourful Kolaba Market, famous for its cut flowers, lay the village of the Kolis where the descendants of the original fishing tribes still lived in reed huts, very much as they had always lived. They were a Marathi-speaking group, the men and women working as partners.

In the dark the men went out in their long narrow open boats, some with raised plank sides, some fitted with outriggers. Most, as in the sketches, had lateen triangular sails with one corner cut off vertically to form a short luff enabling them to sail into the wind. The one-masted sails could be reefed or lowered in seconds when a hefty gale struck. These locally-made clipper-bowed boats could also, when becalmed or if the slanting masts snapped, easily be rowed. The nets were pulled in at dawn, and in the early light a fleet of these little craft made a fairy-tale picture, the first rays of the sun turning their patched sails to gold as they entered the harbour with their catch.

A whopping *wahoo*, such as the woman in the picture is carrying was a prize indeed, one that could be from thirty to sixty inches long. While her husband, wearing a decorative silver belt holding his *langhoti* (loincloth), drags the net up the beach, she carries the *wahoo* with easy pride on a cutting board on which rests a basket too small for the monster. It was not unusual to see a large crow sitting atop all having a meal! This fine woman striding along like a man is wearing her saree Maharashtrian

fashion, the way the hardy Marathi women of old wore them in war when riding a horse. The folds were wound round and pulled tightly between the legs to be tucked and knotted at the waist behind. Considering that most sarees were six yards in length they made extraordinarily neat and effective trousers. The saree was also worn this way by women working inland in paddy fields.

The sketch at the top vividly shows the Koli in action from the shore. The net was weighted

CECIL ELGEE.

at the edges, folded in a certain way and expertly thrown like a billowing parachute, to land in a circle on the water and rapidly sink. The fisherman then drew it in by the connecting rope in his hand, the *chatti* (pot) at his back handy for this small-fry catch.

The woman's hair is tied back sleekly into a bun, a sweet-smelling frangipani flower or a hibiscus tucked into it as if she were going to a party. Instead, her day was just beginning as she met her husband on the beach and took the fish to market and expertly cut it up. She also prepared and sold Bombay Duck, the small *bombloe* which was dried to a rag in the sun

and served with curry, smelling to high heaven. Afterwards she went home to count the money, cook, and look after her family as well as helping to mend the nets. She was the one who did all the marketing and who firmly held the purse strings, which smelt vilely of fish—as she herself did.

The Kolis were a gay and sociable people enjoying festivals and family weddings. For these occasions the women bathed and wore their sarees fully draped—yet how the scaly smell persisted. There was a saying in Bombay: 'Never ask for change from a Koli woman, and keep upwind of her if you can!'

Praboos and Babus

Praboo is a title of respect meaning Lord or Master, used for well-educated superior persons, and none was more superior than the stout gentleman on the left of the picture carrying book and file, a *chutta* hooked over his wrist. An umbrella was as much a part of uniform to the men of Bombay as was the rolled umbrella to the London City man.

This well-to-do man was very likely a *shroff*, a banker, a man also known as a money lender (though of a very different type and standing from the *bunniya* (corn merchant) that name brings to mind, who plied his trade in the smaller towns and held whole families in bondage for generations). This *shroff* was a Brahmin of high-caste priestly descent wearing the Brahmin's sash.

Quietly listening in the middle stands a Bhattia, a dignified and shrewd commercial man of mixed descent from Gujarat, at that time part of the Bombay Presidency. Without being arrogant he would consider himself to be 'better than most', being descended from the Rajputs who had spread over his peninsula centuries before. Certainly he would have felt 'better' than the talkative Bengali *babu* accountant on the right who had come across India from Calcutta.

Bright sock suspenders were as common a sight in India as black umbrellas. If one wore a

dhoti they showed for sure, and no one would have remarked on them—except perhaps to admire their colour.

All day this good-natured, friendly little bandy-legged senior babu with the sock suspenders and the shining pumps sat on a high stool in his office. With a heavy ledger in front of him and peering short-sightedly through his rimless spectacles, he dipped and re-dipped his nib into black ink, scratching away in meticulous script. Many were the tales of the babu's expertise with figures, and so fabulous his memory that on occasions of disasters when the books were lost or burnt, he could reconstruct whole columns from memory.

He spoke in a precise English and liked nothing better than to display a use of metaphors. One story ran that when asked how he managed to balance such complicated books and account for every anna, he replied, 'Sir, anna is like pearrl. Sometime diver comes up with one, sometime he does not, thus, your honour, I go on diving till I find that pearrlee anna!'

CECIL ELGEE.

A Praboo Lady

This wealthy Marathi-speaking lady was most likely the wife of the Praboo 'Lord' we have just seen, and a charming picture she and her daughter make admiring the butterflies fluttering above the canna lilies in her garden. She is wearing a fine silk *choli* (blouse) and *marvad* (pyjamas) over which she has draped a shortish saree in the usual way—over her left shoulder so that the right hand can adjust it. In Bombay Gujarati women (for example, a Bhattia wife) were distinguishable by the way they wore their sarees over their right shoulders.

The Praboo's wife here wears a wooden comb in her hair which (like the humble Koli woman) she has adorned with a flower. Both mother and daughter wear the red *tilak* spot on their foreheads. Also like the Koli women, the Praboo lady could be sniffed a *kos* (two miles) away, in this case most pleasantly, she being heavily scented with musk perfume.

In the sketch at the top her children have rushed out to meet the toy vendor appearing outside their gate selling balloons, miniature boats, birds and windmills on sticks which gyrate rushingly when held up in a wind.

Below, the Hindu lady is seen at the temple near her home performing her *puja* (prayers) before the god's images. The man–woman *lingam-i-yoni* represents Creation, the sacred symbol of Siva, god of the Hindu Trinity. Nandi, a sacred bull, is Siva's mount. Her offerings, placed before these symbols, were

sweetmeats, fruits and flowers or marigold petals, some of which she scatters on the plinth.

Like her husband she believed in the doctrine of *karma* where the soul is eternal and pre-destined to experience many births and deaths. Her calendar was full of Hindu festivals to celebrate: the Divali, festival of lights; the Ganesh Chaturthi, birthday of the elephant god Ganapati; Holi, in spring where coloured water and powder is thrown; and the Rama Navani, celebrating the birth of Rama. The Hindu lady's life was very full—she always rose early to go to the temple after bathing, coming back to supervise the running of her house and her large family swollen by hangers-on, *cha-laoing* (ordering about) her many servants, and last but not least pleasing her husband.

At the age of about fourteen she moved into her husband's home as a bride after an arranged marriage, which, in the way of arranged marriages, turned out well after a sticky start. The sticky start was not due to the fault of the handsome slim young bridegroom with good prospects in the business world, but because of his domineering mother and jealous sisters ruling the roost. But the bride knew that with patience she would be accepted after bearing a son; and one day *she* would become the matriarch.

CECIL ELGEE.

Bombay Buttercups

This was the name by which the traffic policemen were known because of their distinctive yellow caps. They stood, as traffic cops all over the world stand, on a raised box in the centre of converging thoroughfares in Bombay their lips pursed in an almost continuous blast of shrill whistles.

How they ever sorted out the chaos of the conglomeration of pedestrians, bicycles, *tongas*, *ekkas*, *gharries*, handcarts, bullock-carts, donkeys, camels, dogs, babies, prams, cows, *dhoolies* and rickshaws was a mystery to all. Yet they did sort them out and get them moving with only the occasional accident—usually when one of the overloaded lorries, top-heavy with cargo for the docks, overturned. There were trams, some buses, and a growing number of taxi-cabs and private cars, but most of the traffic was on foot, on bicycles, or in horse-drawn conveyances when this picture was painted.

The Bombay Buttercup's problems in those days came from the pandemonium as carts tipped up spilling their pomegranates, jack-fruit, melons and mangoes in rolling heaps, bicycles skidded to avoid meandering cows, horses sat down in their traces, and a pair of oxen yoked together dug in their hooves and refused to budge however much their driver, swathed in a cotton sheet and squatting on the pole-bar, belaboured his beasts and twisted their tails. It was then that the Bombay Buttercup lost his cool and, spitting out his whistle, let fly a string of quite unprintable words.

The *tonga* was the most useful and most over-worked vehicle of the lot. Its seats athwart crammed with humanity, this rickety two-wheeled trap was drawn by a skinny pony whipped into sluggish action by the *tonga-wallah* on his perch. An *ekka* was a smaller one-horse or one-person vehicle with a canopy; a *gharrie* a larger four-wheeled carriage like a Victoria, often with pram-hood as in the sketch. Behind the *gharrie*, and exactly drawn, are the Municipal Offices where the babus plied their pens. Lockwood Kipling, illustrator and sculptor who worked at the Bombay School of Art, father of the famous Rudyard, was responsible for the decorations round this building, in keeping with Bombay's ornate architectural style.

At the top of the page is a Mussalman policeman, truncheon ready to hand. When

CECIL ELGEE.

sent out on riot control he carried a *lathi*, a brass or iron-bound bamboo stave, a most effective weapon when brought down sharply on toes (usually bare) or used horizontally to strike the shoulders or heads of an aggressive mob.

Rioting was usually of a communal nature, Muslim versus Hindu and vice versa depending on the provocation. The very rumour that someone had let loose an unclean animal in the precincts of a mosque (especially at festival time) was enough to set these principal communities at each other's throats. A pig was anathema to a Muslim, the word *soo'r* so detestable and defiling that in conversation they would never use it. Thus when the tale of the supposed sighting of an unclean animal gained credence, the crowds gathered, the opposing sides screamed abuse at each other while throwing missiles, and the staunch police, both Hindu and Mussalman, arrived at the double and let fly with their *lathis*, keeping the factions apart till tempers abated. Then, with only a few broken heads and a few broken feet to show for it, life in Bombay resumed its normal tenor.

The Interview

At first glance this picture shows three dissimilar figures, one of whom is reading a document, meeting in a bare-boarded room. On closer inspection it tells a story which was constantly enacted all over India.

The Punjabi Mussalman on the right (or PM as they were known) had applied for the job of *chowkidar* (watchman) to a firm or a government office. It must have been a large institution to employ a *chuprassi* (messenger) as important as this one in his red uniform with badge of office grandly slung from the shoulder. His white hairs show him to be man of much experience, and a senior one too, by his sergeant's stripes. He was in fact the linchpin of the whole affair.

The PM looks like an ex-sepoy (soldier), and as such stood a very good chance of getting the job. Ex-sepoys could always be recognized in a crowd by their upright bearing, and this PM wears his *pugri* with such extra flair, his *silwar* (trousers) are made up from yards and yards of such pristine fine cotton, and his *gurgabi* (toe-turned-up shoes) are so elegant that even the formidable *chuprassi* must have been impressed, comparing him favourably with the Bombay riff-raff who had already applied for the post.

Normally a sepoy enlisted in the Indian Army for a fifteen-year stretch, at the end of which he retired with a small pension to his smallholding in his village. Sometimes he found he could not make both ends meet what with his debts to the *bunniya* and his crops failing, so he left his land to be tilled by a coolie and came to the city seeking work, bringing his wife and young son—as in the sketch on the left. She was a Punjabi woman dressed in a long *kamiz* slit at the sides and with a *duputta* over her head.

Whatever the circumstances the PM was keen to get this job when he handed his application form to the *chuprassi* on the steps of the building. Coins changed hands and he was bidden to wait—a long wait—but that was normal: nothing was ever done in a hurry. Eventually the *chuprassi* conducted him into the building to meet the babu in the empty outer room where the latter studied the application while the *chuprassi* stood by holding a sheaf of personal *chits* (references).

CECIL ELGEE.

The letter-writer sketched on the left is very much part of this little tale, for our PM could not write English. It was monsoon time, so the *munshi* (as letter-writers as well as teachers and secretaries were called) sat on a brick to raise himself above the puddles, his broken-winged umbrella dripping wetly as his ink-stained fingers pressed nib to paper. That he was kept hard at it on the kerbside and made a good living was not surprising, since the greater part of the inhabitants of Bombay, as well as those in the rest of the country, were illiterate.

With any luck, and with the oiling of further palms, the PM would be ushered into the presence of the sahib himself, with whom he would be quite at ease having known many such in the army, answering his questions smartly and looking him straight in the eye. He would then be dismissed and told to wait outside while the sahib made up his mind.

In this instance the PM probably paid the letter-writer to compose and transcribe the application for the *chowkidar's* job, he signing his name in Urdu at the bottom. Moreover, for a further sum, the scribe could well have written some of the personal recommendations, inventing some likely addresses and signatures. All in all landing a job needed a lot of forethought and could be quite a costly business. I hope he got it!

Parsis

The odd man out here is the stout little Madrassi bearer on the right waiting for the two Parsi gentlemen to finish their conversation before conducting them into the house. The Parsi on the left wears a brown new-style cap, while the thin older man wears the old-fashioned cap, usually maroon in colour, and is of the generation that often still wore goatee beards. But though some Parsis may have been more modern than others, they all firmly kept to their old faith.

That was Zoroastrianism, founded by the prophet Zoroaster who was born in AD 660 in Persia, 'Parsi' meaning 'from the City of Pars'. They were monotheistic, worshipping their one god in the agents of purity: earth, sun, fire, water. Following this path of 'Asha', of goodness, centuries ago they were forced to leave their homeland to escape Muslim persecution, suffering many vicissitudes and living at one time on a remote island in the Arabian Sea.

The small, tightly-knit group that survived eventually ended up in Bombay. Their high-principled and benevolent menfolk became leading businessmen and did much to build up commerce in the growing port, particularly in the cotton mills and shipping industries, and in the process most became rich themselves. Between the First and Second World Wars they could regularly be seen down on the beach opening up and laying out their handkerchiefs

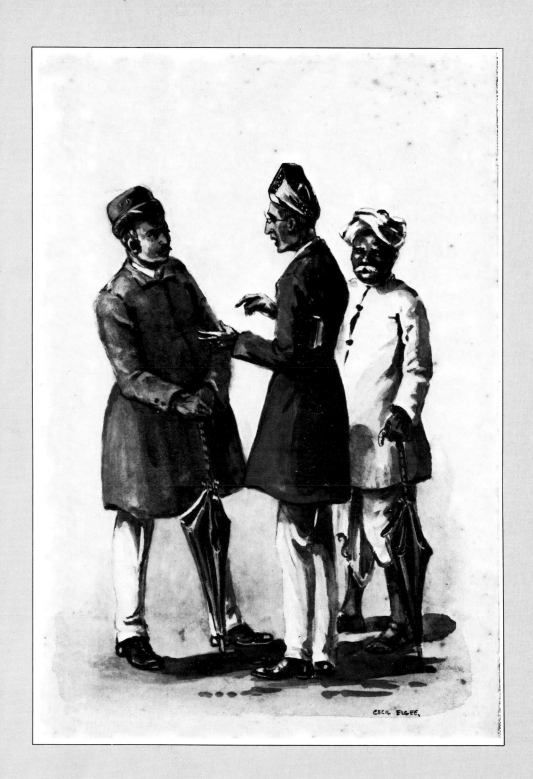

CECIL ELGEE.

carried a corpse to the top of a tower, laid it out on a grid and left it to the vultures waiting in the nearby palm trees. Immediately, with a great flapping of wings the bedraggled grey-feathered griffons swooped and settled, curved claws gripping, and in a tearing of flesh by hooked beaks they devoured the remains, red necks scraggy as they gulped and gorged. Some days later the bones fell through the bars into the pit beneath.

To the humane entrepreneur Parsi, distinguished for his education and wealth, this way of disposing of their people's bodies seemed not ghoulish, but a sensible one to get rid of decaying flesh without defiling the earth, fire or sea.

A delightful story used to be told about how these philanthropic people came to live on the mainland of India in about AD 766. When after their wanderings they asked to be allowed to settle on the peninsula of Gujarat, the King was hesitant. They had enough people in his kingdom already, he said, sending for an earthenware *chatti* of milk (Gujarat was always a great dairy centre) full to the brim to show them just how full up they were. Very carefully one of the Parsis slipped a golden coin into the milk without spilling a drop. So impressed was the King by this feat that he allowed them to stay.

and untying and retying their *kustis* (sacred girdles) while they intoned their prayers and bowed to the sun and the water in an ancient ritual.

The Parsi respected God's earth too much to pollute it with his dead; rich and not-so-rich bodies alike were taken beyond the Hanging Gardens to the Dakhma Towers of Silence to be disposed of. There in a park surrounded by a high wall—for even close relatives were not allowed to see the dreadful end—funerary bearers

A Parsi Lady and her Children

What a pretty picture the Parsi lady makes with her children out for a walk on the *maidan*—any flat open space, a cricket ground, or parade ground. The Law Courts and the Rajabai Tower, from which there was a panoramic view of Bombay, are seen in the background of the sketch over the page. On the *maidan* the Parsi ladies met and chatted together while their children played ball and romped.

The women liked to be Westernized, dressing their children in smocked frocks, knickerbockers, white socks and shoes, the boys often in shorts. The lady here carries a protective sunshade, priding herself on her fair skin which she preserved with great care. 'After all,' she was likely to explain to a guest exclaiming on

the whiteness of her skin, 'After all, we *are* half Greek, you know.' And when the visitor looked bemused at this: 'Yes, the Greeks conquered our land of Persia resulting in much intermarrying.'

That was in Alexander the Great's time, over two thousand years before! By the twenties the Parsis had long become true Bombayites, the ladies wearing their trimmed sarees draped in the Gujarati right-shoulder style, though they wore modern shoes in the latest fashion. They were a colourful community contributing much to the brightness and riches of Bombay, theirs some of the most opulent houses up Malabar Hill—houses built in the style of Scottish mansions or French châteaux, their gardens

CECIL ELGEE.

with 'English' herbaceous borders and sunken gardens filled with statuettes as the roses didn't do too well.

Their hospitality was such that if anyone wanted to raise money for charity the Parsi ladies were approached, their houses thrown open 'by invitation', and there was nothing nicer than to be invited to a Parsi lady's house for tea, provided one had advance warning and had foregone lunch.

In a large drawing-room stuffed with carved blackwood furniture there would be little tables, and chairs in rows against massive cabinets displaying glass and porcelain; it was all delightful. Tea was served from a silver teapot resting on a silver tray, strainer to hand, the cups patriotically decorated with the King Emperor's head. And the food! Delicious well-peppered cucumber sandwiches, fried curry puffs, little iced cakes in bright colours, with Dundee cake to finish.

At these tea parties the Parsi ladies seemed to me to be slightly worried that perhaps everything was not quite *comme il faut*. But they needn't have worried—it always was, and the only thing that was missing to my mind after that large tea was, 'Who's for tennis?'

Ayah with Parsi Baby

The wealthy Parsi lady would have employed an ayah to look after her children, and perhaps one for herself to wash her smalls (the *dhobi* always ruined them), make her bed, brush her hair, and generally care for her personally.

Children's ayahs were perhaps the most beloved by the British of all the servants. They were gentle and kind and faithful—and they spoilt their charges abominably. When the parents were out late Ayah slept by the cot-side on a mat, wrapped up in her cotton saree, guarding the baby. There was a bed, but she would never use it. When the parents returned she would wake instantly, leap to her feet to give the *namaste* bow with clasped hands, before waddling off in the compound to her quarters with her husband and children.

Occasionally one heard of 'bad' ayahs who put opium under their fingernails and let the babies suck them to ensure that they, the ayahs, got a good night's sleep. These women must have been ill or exhausted and beyond their tether, and even they would never have been unkind. The children, when older, very often took it out on the ayah, the boys teasing her, the girls pinching her. Yet she did not 'split' on them (it would have been better sometimes if she had!), never complained and was always serene and reliable.

Of course the mem-sahib would not have approved of many things that went on when her children were left in the ayah's care, had she known about them. For instance she probably never knew that her ayah, as in the sketch,

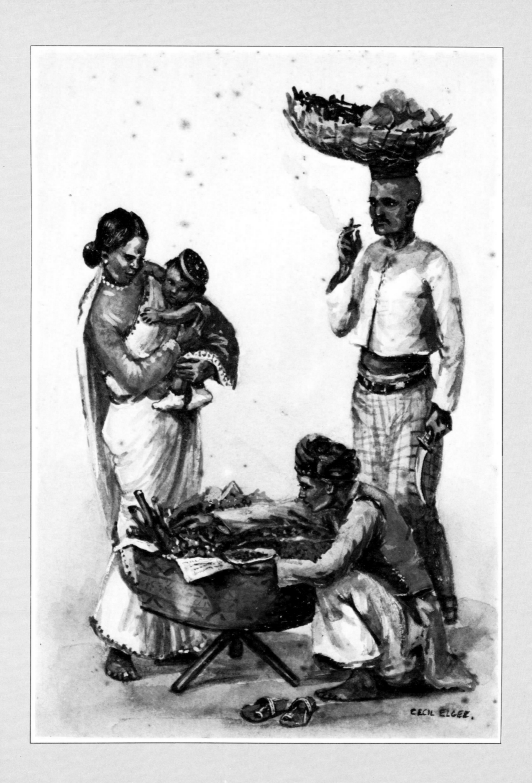

employed a *chokra* (boy) to push the baby's pram when out for a walk. If she had known this it might have brought it home to her that poor Ayah was getting fat and old and needed a younger person to help with the growing family. Certainly if the mem-sahib had known the ayah was taking her baby to the bazaar and giving him sweets from the *mithai-wallah* (sweet-seller) as in the picture, she would have had a fit!

It might be all right for the bouncing Parsi baby seen here squirming eagerly in the ayah's arms to get at the succulent *jilabis*, the sticky pink *shirinis*, the *bhel-puri* and the delicious *chikkis* made of *gur* (raw sugar) and nuts, but these fly-ridden goodies and the dirty paper they were wrapped in were an almost sure source of trouble to white babies. Despite a certain amount of inbreeding Parsis were an exceptionally healthy lot. They were not permitted to

marry outside their religion and were a comparatively small group.

The watching coconut-hawker, wearing an ankle-length *lunghi*, has his basket cleverly balanced with the remaining nuts piled to one side so that any would-be buyer can see what he has to sell. He could shin up palm trees as easily as if there were steps, to deftly cut down his wares with his curved *chakku*. He was a dark-skinned man, a Tamil speaker from the Kerala coast.

There was a pitfall to those new to the country. Many British employed an Anglo-Indian (Eurasian) nanny, her skin—especially if she came from Ceylon (now Sri Lanka)—often darker than the ayah under-nurse who did the washing and stood in on the nanny's day off. Naturally no Anglo-Indian, however far away her European parentage, liked to be taken for an uneducated Indian ayah, any more than a Parsi lady would have liked to have been taken for a poor Hindu woman. When one unwitting Englishwoman addressed her nanny as 'Ayah', she was sharply reminded that not only did she wear shoes and stockings, she also wore a hat for church and smart occasions!

Anglo-Indian nannies too were dearly loved. They were better disciplinarians, and they could read to the children and give them lessons, but there is no doubt in my mind at least that it was the faithful ayahs, who would (and many did) give up their lives to save their charges, who were loved best of all.

Borah Merchants

Here are more of the well-to-do characters to be seen in Bombay. They were the Borah traders, thrifty men of affairs. The Kojah on the left of the picture, on going into his curio dealer's shop, removed his smart buttoned boots, took off his coat and put on an embroidered waistcoat and pillbox hat. Then, squatting on a valuable carpet, he settled down to tot up his takings, rubbing his hands in secret relish at the satisfactory profit, an amount he would never admit to.

He made his money through selling *objets d'art*: folding gate-legged ivory-inlaid tables with separate brass tops, flat-topped elephant tables, Tibetan tea-kettles, carpets, sandalwood boxes, jade ornaments, purdah curtains. He also hired out furniture to the British, but most of all he made his money from silk—valuable silk for cushions, sarees and wedding garments, bales of glowing silk exported to the capitals of Europe.

The Borahs were of various Muslim sects, the

CECIL ELGEE.

Kojah who owned the curio shop being a follower of the Aga Khan from Kirkee near Poona, up in the hills east of Bombay where the Aga had a palace. This 'Great Lord' was the Imam or spiritual leader of the Ismaili sect of the Shi'ite Muslims, the title acquired from the Persian Court. Once a year in Bombay, on outsize scales, there took place the ceremony of balancing his weight against gold, amidst much pomp and speculation. The pomp was only natural in honour of their spiritual and temporal leader; the speculation was as to whether the Aga Khan, already a burly man, had put on weight in the last year, every ounce a bonus as the gold was translated into cash and distributed to the poor. The ceremony originated as a way of gaining revenues for the sect and its leader, the custom continuing as a benevolent gesture.

The enormous gentleman propping himself up with his umbrella in the picture was a Sunni—

another Muslim sect, one at loggerheads with the Shi'ites. This schism, apparent to this day, dated back to mediaeval times, each claiming descent from the Prophet and contesting each other's right to spiritual authority, though all were devout believers in Islam.

'There is no God but God, and Mohammed is his prophet' was the profession of the Borah merchants' faith. Whatever their sect, on the call to prayer from the muezzin atop a minaret, they removed their shoes, leaving them in tidy ranks on the steps of one of their beautiful mosques, did their ablutions in the tank set on the mosaic-paved terrace, and then knelt, stood, and knelt forwards again to pray five times a day. In the annual weeks of Ramadan even our fat Sunni gentleman would not have allowed food or water to touch his lips during the fasting period between sunrise and sunset.

A Mohammedan Woman and her Children

In India kite-flying was tremendously popular, whole families going out to fly them in high places on windy days.

The children in the sketch were from a middle-class family as can be seen from their pretty clothes and also from the fact that their mother is in purdah—'behind the curtain or veil'. They would have bought their kite, while countless barefoot ragged children would have scrounged paper and string and made their own, having just as much fun flying them from the flat roofs of their mud-walled houses as the richer children did.

CECIL ELGEE.

The Mohammedan woman could well have been a wife of one of the Borah merchants on the previous page—seen dressed in her *pājamas* and *kamiz* under a brocaded waistcoat with a long wide mantle over her head, worn only when in her house or about her secluded garden.

Whenever outside she was completely enveloped in the *bourka* from head to foot—as in the sketch opposite—peeping at the half-hidden outside world through square-mesh patches over her eyes. It was stiflingly hot and difficult to breathe under the heavy cotton tent-like affair in the hot weather, yet she would not have been without its privacy and protection. Under it she could go about her business safe from peering eyes; no man would molest her or even look twice at her in her *bourka*. Without it she felt naked—exposed.

Her less well-off sisters, the mass of humble Mohammedan women, were not in purdah—how could they be with their hard lives, working all day in the fields, as coolies on the roads, drawing the water at the wells and grinding the corn? They stayed outdoors together in groups, and if a man appeared nearby and seemed to be eyeing them they drew their *duputtas* swiftly across their faces.

Originally there was no purdah for Hindu women but after the Moghuls conquered India in the sixteenth century the Muslim custom became widespread in middle-class and royal circles. No men were more fiercely protective of their womenfolk than the Rajput princes. Tales were told of lost heads (literally) of courtiers who had dared to look at one of the wives from the *zenana* quarters where the women lived separately—there was even a story of one aspiring princeling losing his head after catching a glimpse of a beauty reflected in a mirror!

The poorer Hindu woman going about her chores in the villages, like her Mohammedan counterpart, drew her saree quickly over her face if there were men about. Often it was said that this drawing of the veil across a woman's face, leaving only the beautiful startled black kohl-lined eyes exposed, was more provocative than if she were walking down the street in next to nothing.

Seen on Hornby Road

Wonderful characters of this kind, though rarer now, can still be seen in Bombay. This man's conical *khulla* (cap) under his turban shows that he was a Muslim. His long matted hair and bushy beard indicate that he was some sort of holy man, a *Haji* perhaps who had made his once-in-a-lifetime pilgrimage to Mecca—but if that were so would he not, as was customary, have dyed his beard red?

Here is a good moment to mention the large *chutta* which appears in so many of these pictures as it did constantly on the streets of India. Forgotten scenes flash to mind, paradoxical, funny settings featuring that all-important and most useful article for rain and shine: a traffic policeman with his umbrella in a belt-harness allowing freedom to his arms; a fisherman with water up to his armpits in the sea holding one up; another of the *mali* (gardener) watering the flowers under one in a shower.

The gentleman in this picture, in his checked apron-skirt, is an eccentric—but not so eccentric that he doesn't carry the ubiquitous umbrella.

Butlers

In smaller establishments they were called simply 'bearers', and they were the head servants, the efficiency with which the household was run greatly depending on their ability. An experienced butler-bearer spoke some English, found and ushered in new servants for the mem-sahib to interview to replace those dismissed or having to go home to their villages to bury a grandfather, uncle, aunt, cousin or nephew. The reasons for a servant having to go home were legion but usually, when it was not for a burial, the roof of his house had fallen in during the monsoon, or he had to marry off a daughter —in which case an advance of some one hundred rupees was requested.

The Hindu butler on the right, carrying in the tray of whisky and soda, was known also as an *abdar* or wine waiter. He wears his sahib's colours in a braid band slashed across his *pugri*, and on a wide cummerbund around his waist. If the master were in the army his regimental colours would be worn thus.

At the top of the page wearing the flat *pugri* is another butler, one from Bengal. The bearer not only carried in the drink tray, but supervised the waiting at table of the *khidmatgars*, and brought in the *chota-hazri* (early morning tea tray)—and it *was* early, at five-thirty or six o'clock so that the sahib could go out riding while it was still cool. He was up first thing in the morning, and to bed the last, always on call for the sahib and mem-sahib, and was more in personal touch with them than any other of the servants.

It was a status symbol to have a Goanese major-domo—such as the butler on the left of the painting carrying a plate of cheese straws on a silver salver—and an even greater one to have a Goanese cook as sketched overleaf. They were the cream of the servants in India, wearing short-jacketed highly-starched white suits and more often than not blancoed plim-soles. They had Portuguese names as de Souza or de Mello, and most of them spoke English as well as other languages.

The culinary artistry of a Goanese cook had to be seen to be believed. He often worked in primitive conditions in tremendous heat, the sweat pouring from him. Once seen and tasted, who could ever forget the dream sweet of home-made ice-cream (there were few fridges but everyone had an icebox) and fresh fruit set in meringue, decorated with a candyfloss of burnt sugar woven into a fairy beehive basket of so delicate a pattern it seemed a crime to break into it? Who can ever forget the excellent pastry, always baked separately like a slab of shortbread, sliding off the pie at table?

These delectable dishes were cooked on a mud-brick stove with one hole in the side, another on top, and a round oven, the whole fired by charcoal. It was the duty of the *mati* to light the stove before daybreak when the *barwachi-khana* (kitchen-room, known coloquially as a *babachi-khana*) became wreathed in smoke, the *mati* vigorously fanning the charcoal in a desperate attempt to get it glowing steadily before he was overcome by the fumes. Cooking was done in gleaming *degchies*—handleless saucepans—which he cleaned by scouring with ashes and sand. As the oven was never big enough, extra baking was done by placing hot coals on the lids, the roast inside the *degchie* sizzling away on the stove.

It was also the *mati*'s job, as in the sketch over the page, to grind on a curry stone spices of peppercorns, green and red chillies, cinnamon, ginger root, cummin seeds, cloves, turmeric and all the other ingredients of curry powder.

CECIL ELGEE.

jharans—thick cotton cloths—for the *dhobi* to collect, the mem-sahib handing out another twelve of these, the necessary daily quota for reasonable cleanliness. If, sensibly, she had no wish to raise her blood pressure, she did not go again into the kitchen until it was tidied up for her inspection next morning. Sufficient to know it was cleared once in twenty-four hours!

The standards of Goanese servants were so high that the inevitable slip-ups that occurred in every household were to them humiliating disasters. I well remember the black-letter day occasion when, at a dinner party given for the Viceroy and his Lady, the perfect and formerly unflappable butler (whose name *was* de Mello), in a fit of nerves, tipped the peas he was holding over the Vicereine's shoulder into her silken lap. There was a thunderous silence round the long, laden, candle-lit table broken by an agonized groan from de Mello, aghast at his *lèse-majesté*. A flashing hand glittering with rings brushed off the offending vegetables, while *khidmatgars* rushed in all directions to fetch pans and brushes and sweep up the bouncing balls from under the table. No one dared so much as titter, though most were bursting to laugh, for it was plain to see that Her Excellency was most definitely *not* amused.

The *barwachi-khana* was a separate room standing some little distance away from the back verandah of the main bungalow, a smoke-grimed, from time-to-time whitewashed, building with one small window high up and a fly-proof door that constantly crashed open and shut. Having handed out the daily stores—kept under padlock in the house—the mem-sahib proceeded to inspect her kitchen, empty except for the *khansama* (cook). The mud-baked floor would have been swept of the nightly invasion of two-inch-long brown cockroaches and the fire would be glowing, though the smoky smell remained. In one corner lay a pile of dirty

The Bhisti

He was the water-carrier and though of low caste he was not despised as some low-caste workers were, rather held dear, for water in a parched land meant more than gold. The word *bhisti* was derived from the Persian *Bihist* meaning Paradise, hence 'an inhabitant of Heaven', and well chosen it was for one who brought to those on the battlefield the cool life-giving drink more precious than nectar. In the Mutiny it was written: 'The *bhisti* showed courage and fidelity in supplying water to the wounded in face of much personal danger.' Worthy praise indeed to the humble water-carrier—'You're a better man than I am, Gunga Din!'

In this sketch, the *bhisti* is seen braking his bullock laden with *mussaks* down a steep slope in the hills around Matheran beyond Bombay. These *mussaks* were made by leather workers, who skinned a goat (or even a buffalo)

CECIL ELGEE

like a rabbit, cutting round the neck and legs so that the hide stayed in one piece with a minimum of holes and no stitching. The projecting stumps were tied with thongs, one thong being used to sling the bag over the shoulder. It was like the biblical wine-skin but larger, slightly porous to keep the water cool by light evaporation. A canvas *chargul* had much the same slight sweating effect—these smaller containers were used when in camp, hung on a branch, the wind keeping them beautifully cool.

To protect himself from the injurious effects of the damp on his skin the *bhisti*, as in the picture, wore a red flannel cummerbund, *cummer* being the Urdu for waist, *bund* for sash. Many people in India right up to the last war copied this idea, believing the sweat round their waists could give them a chill or even cholera (an earlier misapprehension), hence the cholera-belt, a knitted cummerbund worn by both men and women.

When the heat of the sun began to wane and the *mali* (gardener), as in the sketch above, tied up some drooping flowers and fetched his can for the evening's watering, the sinewy-legged *bhisti* went round the house with his *mussak*, spraying the ground to lay the dust. In the tremendous heat of April, May and June before the monsoon broke, he would at intervals through the day spray the verandahs that shaded and surrounded most bungalows, at the same time sluicing down the *kuss-kuss tatties* of grass matting hanging over doors. It cooled the air appreciably and had the added bonus of wafting the pleasant scent of the *kuss-kuss* roots through the stuffy house.

The most important duty of the *bhisti* was attending to the water in the bathrooms *en suite* to each bedroom. It sounds modern, even luxurious, to have a bathroom each, but it was by no means so, for there was no plumbing in India other than in large towns, and upcountry there would be only one outside tap for the whole compound.

The *ghussal-khana* (bathroom) with one door from the bedroom and another to the compound, was a box-like room with concreted floor and no window. In one corner stood the commode— commonly known as a 'thunder-box'—and a

table with *chilumchi* (basin) and jug of water. Another corner was enclosed by a few inches of raised concrete, the floor sloping to a hole in the wall through which the dirty water ran out when the zinc tub was tipped up. Through this hole snakes were apt to venture, attracted by the damp coolness of the floor, lurking unseen in the dimness, and many were the stories of sahibs and evil snakes confronting each other over the bathtub. The answer was to bung up the holes with chicken-wire and the *bhisti* checked that these had not been dislodged, searched for scorpions and saw that the large earthenware jars were full of cold water. He then went outside and squatted by his wood fire in the compound where his kerosene tins of water were heating, waiting for one of the most familiar cries of the days of the Raj.

'*Ghussal jaldi lao*, bring bath quickly,' shouted the bearer when the sahib indicated he was ready.

'*Ghussal tiar hai, huzoor!*' came the joyful, ready answer from the *bhisti*, jumping to his feet and staggering into the bathroom with his boiling kerosene tins, and pouring them into the tub.

The *mali* planted his salvias, marigolds and geraniums in straight rows and then watered them; the *bhisti* would not water the paths— that was the *mali*'s job—and neither of them would wet their hands washing the dirty dishes. For that task a *masalchi* was employed.

The compound was full of these different servants of rigid caste system, none doing more than his allotted-in-life task. They lived in flat-roofed outhouse quarters with their families in the larger stony-earthed area at the back of the house away from the formal garden to the front, the whole surrounded by a low white wall. It hummed with life and drama—cooking fires, *hookhas*, children and flies, the bearer keeping an eagle eye out for misbehaviour, the mem-sahib handing out extra clothes and blankets in winter, advising the women over hygiene, and treating any mild ailments. It was a village in itself.

The Dhobi

What pride this *dhobi* took in his beast of burden! How carefully he fed and groomed him, the bullock's head decorated with beads and tassels, his horns gold-tipped, his hooves polished, the bag carrying the clean washing gay with multicoloured patches.

Not only did this *dhobi* take pride in his bullock, but he took care of his own appearance, wearing silver bangles on his ankles and wrists, dangling earrings in his ears, a clean Marathi-type flat *pugri* on his head. He was from the western state of Katiawar, across the Bay of

Cambry, a land of fertile fields where the farmers were clad in white homespun cotton and the women in full red skirts, a land that to the north bordered on Sind and Rajputana.

More usual was the sight of a *dhobi* with a donkey or a clapped-out bicycle, the bundle resting on the saddle and handlebars; but wherever they were and however they looked they all had learnt their skills from their fathers, handed down through generations of *dhobis*, their greatest pride to return the dirty wash clean, bleached, starched, ironed, and expertly folded—often on the same day.

Few *dhobis* lived in the compounds. Daily they set forth from their homes by the bazaars to collect the laundry and take it down to the river. Hitching up their *dhotis* and taking off their *pugris*—leaving exposed their topknots (by which they could be pulled up to heaven when they died)—they set to with a will. As in the sketch they bashed and slammed and hit the garments on smooth rocks, then rubbed them forcefully with long bars of yellow soap called *saboon*, a word derived from the French *savon*. After more bashings and great rinsings the clothes were laid out to dry on the banks of the river before being taken to a small smoky room where, with a charcoal iron on a table, miracles were wrought with scarcely a smut to show.

Even more miraculous was the starching. It was the days when boiled shirts were *de rigueur* for gentlemen's evening wear, the fronts required to be as stiff as boards. This the *dhobi*

did with a mixture of rice starch for stiffening and borax for glazing. After boiling the rice he rolled it into a ball and squeezed it through a cloth, using it so copiously on napkins and tablecloths that they were with difficulty peeled open. His method of damping down the clothes for ironing was singular: taking a mouthful of water and a deep breath, he sprayed them accurately through the gaps in his teeth.

Ah! *Dhobi-ji* (the suffix 'ji' was a mark of affection and respect)—how wonderfully you coped under the circumstances. It was no wonder the clothes smelt of your wood smoke, no wonder with all that bashing to get them clean that the rate of wearing out was phenomenal. No wonder the mem-sahib washed her silk stockings, crêpe-de-Chine camiknicks and chiffon blouses in the *chilumchi* in her own dark bathroom—just think what *they* would have looked like had she left them to you!

Sweepers

The sweepers, who were known as *bhangis* or *mehtas*, were the lowest of the low, the poorest, the worst paid, a caste in Coventry, not one to have contact with—in fact the untouchables. It was not until Mahatma Gandhi in his compassion brought their status to the public eye that anyone noticed or thought about them at all. Yet they were a responsible, kindly, long-suffering people, and they were an indispensable part of life in India. They dealt with the night

soil when the only drains were the rivers, the canals, the ditches, the very gutters running down each side of the muddy streets.

They were also tenders of parks and cemeteries and cleaners of outside places—unlike the *hamal* in the sketch over the page raising the dust as he dusted, who was a cut above, and could clean *inside* the house.

Bhangis swept the roads and the paths with their twig brooms—the sahibs nicknamed them

CECIL ELGEE.

next 'visit'. His buckets were emptied into round tin containers at the back of the compound, and a foul-smelling buffalo cart came to collect them.

He knew more about the state of the household's health than the people concerned did themselves, dysentery and other horrible infections being easy to diagnose, and he was quite liable to spread it round the compound that the mem-sahib was going to have a baby before she had really grasped the fact herself, which was maddening when they all smiled smugly as if they knew (which they did) when the happy fact was proudly announced.

'the knights of the broom'. A woman sweeper carried a variety of baskets in which to put the rubbish, balancing them one on top of the other as easily as a trained juggler, her bearing that of a princess. Indeed she was called a princess: a *mehtrani*! Was this sarcasm a tongue-in-cheek jibe at the expense of the poor sweeper-*lōg*, or were they after all as appreciated as the water-carrier 'man from Heaven' was?

Whatever the answer the *mehta* was a necessary part of the scene, and though humbler even than the *bhisti* and the *dhobi* he was often more knowledgeable. He was never off duty in the sahib's compound, always there ready, squatting on his hunkers, waiting, his bright black eyes watching, his ears listening to the sounds that told him it was time to go and empty the 'thunder-box' again. A dozen times a day a *mehta* did this, pouring in creosote oil, leaving it spruce in its smell of coal tar, ready for the

Pathan Chowkidar

There was another indispensable character who lived and worked in the compound of the sahib's house: the night watchman. He was a deterrent and insurance against thieves and those who did not employ a *chowkidar* laid themselves open to trouble.

This striking figure of a bearded Mussalman, wearing the blue *pugri* of the Afghan with beautiful flowing *shamla* and ornate leather

chupplis (sandals), and carrying a stout *lathi* such as the riot police used, came from across the border one winter to seek work, rather as the Punjabi Mussalman on page 30 came to Bombay. Times were always hard where he lived in the rugged mountains, and that summer had been harder than most. He badly needed money and, drifting southward, found employment in the cantonment town of Poona.

CECIL ELGEE.

Unlike the Punjabi this tribesman did not bring his wife. He had left her to guard his interests, using his old matchlock *jezail* if necessary—she was almost as fine a shot as he! 'Allah help the Pathan who draws his wife's fury upon his own head' was a well-known saying in those parts.

He had left with a brother his prized Enfield, a rifle he had taken from the British encamped in the Kajuri Plain on the boundaries of the Tribal Territories—a huge bolster of land running from Baluchistan to Kashmir. The tribesmen made them in an open-fronted shop known as the Kohat Rifle Factory (though it was well outside that town), the fitters copying captured rifles in detail down to the serial numbers—but his was not a copy: it was the real thing.

It was a court-martial offence in the Indian Army for a sepoy to lose his rifle which in camp was secured by a loose chain round his waist as he slept. On a dark night, near-naked and oiled all over, the Pathan had slipped through the barbed wire surrounding the camp, slithered over the low stone wall, crawled under a tent flap, found a carelessly unattached rifle, and got away without so much as a sentry stirring.

Now without his rifle he felt bereft, but he did not intend to stay in Poona more than one winter. He had other ways of making money, and his job as the Captain-sahib's *chowkidar* would guarantee immunity from suspicion. Besides he would serve the Captain-sahib well, for was he not in his pay, had he not taken his salt?

That winter things went well with the *chowkidar* and he was pleased. The Captain was pleased too. He was also an experienced Frontier man, displaying a green and navy medal ribbon on his chest. He spoke Pashtu, the language of Afghanistan and the Frontier, with his new night-watchman, and prided himself that he knew all about the unruly, likeable Pathan.

The Captain knew only too well that a camel train coming down a narrow pass (as in the sketch) could well be not as innocent as it looked. When he was out on the Kurram Pass, he had seen one approaching, but as the train neared his patrol the tribesmen grabbed rifles hidden under the bundles and disappeared behind rocks to fire on them at unpleasantly close quarters, the camels scattering off in alarm at the rat-tat-tat of shots, to gather in a haughty group below the pass.

Well he knew they could be up to anything, but his Pathan *chowkidar* worked admirably night after night doing his rounds with hurricane *butti* lifted, peering in to black corners, his *lathi* at the ready, before settling down on the front verandah and wrapping himself up against the cold of winter. Of course he slept. He could be heard snoring in the night; what *chowkidar* didn't? Every morning as the Captain strode out early to the waiting *syce* holding his horse, he glanced along the verandah and saw that the *chowkidar* had left for his quarters right at the back by the compound wall. He was such an excellent watchmen that there were no thefts or even attempted thefts from their bungalow that winter though there seemed to be an inordinate amount of them in the rest of Poona.

One day when the nights were no longer cold and the weather was beginning to hot up unpleasantly, the police came round to the Captain's house. They had at last traced the leader of the gang of thieves which had made more trouble that winter than all the other winters put together.

The *chowkidar's* go-down was empty except for a tidy pile of blankets on the *charpoy* (string-bed) and the sahib's hurricane *butti* in a corner. The bird, much to the police inspector's disgust, had flown. Secretly the Captain was rather glad.

A Travelling Circus

It sent shivers up the spine to watch a snake-charmer playing his pipe, the snake waking from his basket, pushing off the lid and swaying from side to side in an undulating dance. In this picture the large vicious-looking snake, held tightly by the charmer, probably had had his fangs removed or the poison had just been withdrawn through a forced bite, though if

CECIL ELGEE.

asked the snake-charmer would stoutly deny this.

Watching as if he has all the time in the world to spare is a coolie carrying a basket of parcels his mem-sahib has told him to collect urgently from the stores. With him is a *chokra* dressed in a white coat with brass buttons employed to take the family dog for a walk, known as dog-boy. Of the onlookers the dog is obviously the most terrified!

The travelling circus went from town to town, to villages, through districts, and to cities, putting on a variety of shows as in the sketches: goats trained to balance, monkeys dressed in skirts and pillbox hats cavorting in comic antics that had the audiences roaring with laughter. There was the noise of drums, fifes and cymbals to attract the attention of the public; there were fortune-tellers, dancing-girls

performing their graceful gyrations, and acrobats crossing wobbly, hastily erected tightropes.

Many clustered round the conjuror as he performed tricks with cards and pulled coloured scarves tied together out of boxes which, when examined, had no false bottoms. But none of these could beat the mango tree trick, and when it was announced that it was about to take place the crowd gathered thickly.

It was an old, old, trick, the secret handed down like most things in India from father to son, intriguing generation after generation, and no one could ever fathom *how* it was done. A mango stone was sown in a flower pot and covered with a large cloth, after which followed an awful lot of legerdemain and patter with lewd jokes thrown in to distract the onlookers who nevertheless kept their eyes glued on the cloth. Incredibly, it shook and rose in height, higher and higher until at last it was whipped off. There, lo and behold, before their very gaze was a perfect miniature mango tree, a real green-leaved tree bearing fruit. It was passed round and sure enough there was a mango hanging from a branch.

Long and loud far into the night the discussion went on as to how the mango trick was done, the people half believing the mango had magical powers. Once a spectator (so the story ran) picked the fruit to examine it closely whereupon he fell sick. He felt so ill he consulted his Brahmin priest who told him his only hope was to restore the mango to its rightful owner, whereupon the poor man staggered from village to village in search of the travelling circus, eventually coming up with them and was restored to health. That, if any proof was needed, showed that there was magic in the mango tree trick!

The Cotton Teaser

In the spinning and weaving industries in the villages of the Katiawar district that bred Gandhi, where cotton grows prolifically, the flock beater was a common sight. He teased the cotton with his *ping-jam*, an onomatopoeic word resembling the sound of the twanging cord. When he teased the cotton it fluffed all over the place in sneeze-making lumps, and he used the red kerchief (attached to the string in the picture) for tying round his nose and mouth.

CECIL ELGEE.

In the sketch on the left, the Katiawari *dhood-wallah* (milkman) was another well-known figure, wearing the cowman's smock in those milk-producing parts not far from where the Parsis landed. He is carrying in earthenware *chattis* which, like the *bhisti's mussaks*, are sufficiently porous to cool milk or water, the curds and the buttermilk, that kept the people there plump and healthy.

The sweet picture shown below shows a child in the exact replica of her mother's dress tending her small floppy-eared sheep in the hills bordering on Rajputana, the sheep so different from the larger fat-tailed *dhumba* to be found further north. She had tended her little sheep since she was old enough to toddle up the hills with her brothers and sisters, thwacking her stick on the ground with cries of '*ah olé*' as she urged the sheep into their pens at night to keep them safe from jackals, hyenas and the prowling panther.

The process of getting the seed out of the cotton (after it was picked from the fields where the rounded bolls looked like lumps of white candyfloss) was a simple one. Sitting on the floor the teaser held his *ping-jam* like a harp, pulling the cotton over the string and letting it go with a thrum, separating the seed from the flock. The flakes of cotton were then collected and spun into thread while the seed was made into flat cakes and fed to cattle.

Convicts in India were given the task of making carpets in the local prisons, cotton druggets known as *dhurries* which made useful and inexpensive floor coverings.

A Kumhar and a Lombadi Woman

The woman is watching the potter create a *chatti*, his artistic hands covered with clay, feeling, lifting, forming, denting, shaping the earthenware pot on his heavy wheel. Every now and then as the wheel slowed down he picked up the stick, inserted it with unerring accuracy into the hole on the edge of the whirling platform

and with a few powerful twists speeded the wheel.

When the *kumhar* felt satisfied with the shape of the pot, he cut it from its twirling base with a wetted string and put it in the sun to dry. Later he baked it in an improvised kiln.

His young assistant took the *chattis* to the

CECIL ELGEE.

bazaar on braying donkeys who were so wickedly obstinate that their noses were bored to make them more amenable. Whatever was the use of throwing pots if they got broken on the way to market when the wretched donkeys bolted and kicked? That really infuriated the old *kumhari-wallah* who fumed and swore he would never make another pot until those donkeys were tamed.

The Lombadis—better known as Banjaras—are a migratory tribe, traders in grain and other foodstuffs, travelling regularly from central to south India in large groups. In earlier days they were notorious thieves, the men stealing cattle, the women stealing children—a reputation hard to live down in more modern times. Local women would take their small children into the house and shut the doors when a caravan of Banjaras was camping nearby.

In contrast to their naked babies the Lombardi women were thickly clad in garments ringed with the colours of the rainbow, with small mirrors let into the cloth. In addition they wore all their worldly goods and dowries in the form of heavy necklaces, earrings, bangles and belts with jewelled ends. Their headpieces were edged with silver fringes so that they flashed, sparkled, reflected and jangled as they moved.

This bare baby had no need of toys. He had a whole range to play with as he sat in his mother's lap—even rings to cut his teeth on!

Women at the Well

The scene is as old as history. Only in the mountains of India are springs and gushing streams to be found, the sources of water for the villagers in the plains being either a river (which, it is hoped, does not fail in the dry season), a tank or a well.

Tanks were, and still are, artificial reservoirs dammed by an earthen *bund*, the tank filling to the brim in the monsoon. Everything and everybody came to the tank to water: buffaloes and pigs wallowed in it; people washed their clothes and themselves in it; mosquitoes bred; *mugger* (blunt-nosed crocodiles) and turtles lurked, and water was drawn from it by the women for domestic use.

There were two main types of well. The village with a well was better off than one with a tank, since it was less liable to dry up. The *bhauri* well had steps down to the water's edge on one side, where the women could bathe in the cool shade of the deep walls in some seclusion before drawing their water. This step-well in action could be heard miles away as yoked bullocks walked up and down a worn path on the other side, a pulley contraption groaning and squeaking when the water was drawn up in a skin.

The most common well, however, was like the one in the picture, parapeted and capped with a well-head gear from which the women let down and pulled up a leather or metal bucket to fill their *chattis* and brass pots.

The three Hindu women in the picture come from various parts of India and have been

length, when washed are laid out to dry on the steps of a tank while the women wash, splash, cluster and chat—beautiful women, with black collyrium from a candle flame and copper rimming their doe eyes. The long strips of deep red sarees drying on the *ghat* steps, their colour reflected in the still water, perhaps an arched bridge in the background, are a gift from the gods to one deft with a paint brush.

It must be one such colourfully dressed wife who is riding in the *ekka*, the *ekka-wallah* taking pride in his well-fed horse trotting out, ears pricked, a plume waving on his head. Exposed as she was to men's gaze on the road, the wife covered her face with her saree, and she could have drawn the curtain hanging from the canopy all round her if she wished for complete privacy.

Grace showed in every line in these diversely dressed women at the well, in their superb carriage as they bore their water home with easy naturalness—the one from Bombay tall, slender and elegant, the one from the United Provinces with stately upright posture, the girl from Rajputana enchantingly supple as she swung along lithely on her bare feet, her solid silver anklets glimpsed with her full skirt swishing and swirling and folding around her in rippling movements.

brought together here at a village well to show the differences in their dress. The woman on the right, carrying the pot with a small *lotah* on top, is recognizable as coming from the Bombay Presidency. The brightly-dressed woman on the left with the half-saree, holding a small *chatti* and wearing a brief *choli* which reveals her midriff, is from the United Provinces; and the girl in the middle is from Rajputana where the colours of the garments are among the gayest and most varied in the whole of India. Their skirts are enormously full, very often of a favoured wine-red shade bordered deeply in turquoise, their short sarees multi-patterned on the same translucent claret background. These sarees, about two and a half yards in

Brassbound Bhil

The Bhils were a primitive people from the Central Provinces, who with the aboriginal Gonds inhabited the ancient state of Malwa where they lived in the mountains and the rich teak forests. They were a wild stocky breed with flat noses, their hair bound back, the men wearing only bright loincloths. They were trackers and hunters, expert with bow and arrow in their terrain of deep rivers and thick undergrowth which concealed tigers and other big game.

Living in the forests and subsisting by the chase, their existence was primaeval, and by the turn of the century they were coming down

into the villages seeking what menial tasks they could get and settling on any land available.

Indulging in excessive tobacco smoking and much strong liquor, these superstitious Hindu primitives, to the high-class Hindu's horror, ate not only the flesh of buffaloes, but of cows. They ranked as unclean leather-working *chamars* who dealt with hides, made *mussaks* and feasted on dead carcasses.

Their great asset when they came to settle—called then Hill-Bhils—was their wives who were hard-working and domesticated, unlike some of the other rude tribes whose women were hunters as tough and warlike as their men. These

CECIL ELGEE.

mented mother was so 'brassbound' that she had to stuff paper and grass down her anklets to prevent them chafing, and on her arms she wore dozens more of these brass bangles. As well as these she wore a jewelled stud in one nostril and in the other an unwieldy nose ornament which was attached by a chain to her silver headband to stop it dragging. Into her dress metal, mica, glass, shells—anything going —was sewn. The whole effect of this tribal costume was of glittering magnificence, her earrings and the silver rings on her toes of solid workmanship and considerable value.

The *chukki* (grindstone) was worked by two women turning the upper stone. Every so often more grain was poured down the centre, coming out round the edge as flour to be swept up. It was a restful, sedentary occupation, which must have been a relief after carrying all that weight around.

characteristics prompted great devotion in their wayward menfolk who gave themselves up and were prepared to die rather than see their wives imprisoned for some crime they very likely had committed themselves under the influence of drink.

The quick-witted, adaptable Hill-Bhil woman carried all her wealth on her (even slept in it), as ornately clothed as her husband was starkly. It was winter when this picture was painted, the toddler wearing his cold-weather clothing which consisted of a warm bonnet and a silver belt dangling a rupee in a strategic spot! His orna-

Ascetics

Once every twelve years there occurred in each of four towns in India, chosen because a drop of immortal nectar fell on them from the sky, a *Kumbh Mela*, a pilgrim fair, to which hundreds of thousands came. Nasik, near Bombay, is one where there was an old Dravidian temple as in the sketch and where 'tiger-men' painted in realistic lime and yellow stripes postured in the suggestive attitudes of temple ritual, while pilgrims made their obeisance to the god's images. Ujjain is another, and Allahabad yet another of these holy cities, as there the Jumna River meets and unites with the Ganges in a most sacred spot named the *Sangam*.

Particularly sacred is the fourth, Hardwar,

the most northern of the towns, at the foot of the Himalayas in the United Provinces. Here is the fount of Hinduism where by a gorge at Gangadwara, the Gate of Ganges, the river bursts out from the mountains at one thousand feet above sea level to widen out, slow down and make her more leisurely way along the twelve hundred miles to the sea.

There, at Hardwar, during the *Mela*, the

population swollen to a near million, the pilgrims move in massed crowds to the holy Mother Ganges. In life, drinking its waters and bathing in it washes away the Hindu's guilt, absolves him from his sins by purifying him, leading nearer to his ultimate goal of no more rebirths but to life eternal in heaven. In death all Hindus wish to be cremated on 'Ganga Mai's' banks, their ashes thrown on to her bosom.

The *Mela* was, and still is, a time of great rejoicing and festivities, drawing on many others to serve the needs of the masses. Food and sweet-meat stalls sold the flat *chappati* unleavened cakes, the drinks, betel-nuts and

CECIL ELGEE

they neared the circular white stone steps that led down to a smallish pool where sacred *mahseer*—the salmon of the Indian river—were fed, some giants as much as thirty to forty pounds in weight. Hari Paki, the holy pool, was thick with bobbing figures reciting their prayers. Women threw rose petals and marigolds into the waters and then discreetly, still in their sarees, immersed themselves, to cure them of all ills and cleanse their souls. Their slender figures were outlined like classic goddesses as wet and dripping they left the water and mounted the steps.

This near-naked *sahdu*, clad only in a strip of cloth and sitting on a panther skin, is smeared all over with burned cow-dung (reputed to keep the wearer warm); his hair a stiff bird's nest of mud, the three-pronged stripes of Siva on his forehead. His Shivite necklace of dark red nutseeds, *rudranghsh*, had the benefit of keeping him in low key: 'lowering his blood pressure' was how it was described to me. Before him lie his religious stock-in-trade: a *bairagi* (crutch) to rest a limb on, the *lotah* or *kamandal* for his food, *chinti* (tongs) with which to make clapping noises. He could also have carried gongs and conch-shells.

Behind him stands a priest in saffron robes, shaven-headed and holding a food bowl. His staff indicates that he is a wandering mendicant proceeding from one festival to another.

The *faqir* is also smeared with ash, his agonized face white with it, his matted hair so long that it hangs like a cord. Attached to his bed is a rope with which his *chela* (disciple) can pull him along. The services of *chelas* are all-important, for as well as growing their hair and beards to enormous lengths, some of these ascetics grow their fingernails so long that they can do little for themselves. Twisted and yellow, their nails look and sound like small, dried-up carob seedpods rattling from the branches of a tree in a wind.

images of deities. There were street shows and entertainments—all the things that went to make up a fair including the clown-man water-seller in the sketch below, his vest and pants in red and white, the holy colours. His feather-ornamented drapes cover *chattis* of holy Ganges water. There were many reasons for buying holy water—one use to 'kill the passion of the lingam'—and in Hardwar it *was* water from the Ganges, but further afield, who could say?

Lining the route to the ritual bathing were many barbers busy with their cut-throat razors shaving the heads of pilgrims, and thick on the ground were the holy men, followers of Vishnu and Śiva, their begging bowls before them, the giving of alms an essential part of the pilgrim's cleansing. Many pilgrims were hurt, and some were trampled underfoot when the crowd gathered momentum, pressing from behind as

The more uncomfortable, the more hurtful, the more the merit. 'That holy man's virtue is very great lying on that bed of nails,' the crowd murmured as they placed money and food by his side. 'If any man deserves eternal nirvana *he* surely does!'

Itmad-ud-Daulah's Tomb

Once upon a time there was a Moghul prince, the great Akbar's son. He was far too high and mighty to ever go shopping, but at an annual fair the ladies of the court set up stalls within the precincts of the palace which lay inside the Agra Fort, and Prince Salim, who was more interested in wine and the arts than in helping his father rule, could indulge in the amusement

of this pastime, highlighted by the bantering and flirtatious atmosphere as he gaily haggled with the veiled ladies selling their wares.

One such lady was the exquisitely lovely Mehr-un-Nissa, daughter of Ghias-ud-din, a Persian from Teheran who had come with his family to India where he had relations at court. Akbar soon recognized Ghias-ud-din's worth, raising him to command a thousand horse and greatly relying on his advice. Now, at the fair, Mehr-un-Nissa's veil slipped, and Prince Salim was so captivated by her looks that he instantly fell in love with her.

But the ways of true love seldom run smoothly and this one certainly didn't, for Mehr-un-Nissa was already betrothed to another. Akbar ensured that she was quickly married to a young Turkoman called Sher Afgan (meaning tiger-thrower), a man of great courage and repute. Moreover the Emperor settled them far away from his son in the district of Malda in Bengal.

Some years later after Akbar the Great had died and Prince Salim had become the Emperor Jahangir, Sher Afgan was killed in a fight with the governor of his province. Rumour was rife that the new emperor had connived at his death. Yet for four years Jahangir avoided the widow, and she lived with the Dowager Empress into whose care she had come, during which time the fame of her beauty and her talents spread through the court and city.

Then, unexpectedly, one day he entered his mother's apartments and saw Mehr-un-din's face again, and found that her charms exceeded even those his imagination had built up over the years. His passion was revived with such intensity that in a few days, with tremendous brilliance, their marriage was celebrated. He called her Nur Jahan, the Light of the World.

He found that she was not only beautiful but had intelligence to match. Jahangir (despite her urging him to take his responsibilities seriously and live in a more sober vein) so admired her accomplishments that he handed over to her the reins of his empire. He was devoted to her statesmanlike father as well, promoting him to the highest ministerial position, that of prime minister and high treasurer, the Itmad-ud-Daulah.

When in 1621 Itmad-ud-Daulah died, the remarkable Queen Nur Jahan had this mausoleum built, her father's mortal remains lying in a marble tomb in the centre of its perfect symmetry. It lies at Agra a few miles north of the Taj Mahal, and indeed though so very much smaller is said to have been the forerunner of the Taj, inspiring Shah Jehan to build that superb monument in memory of his Muntaz Mahal, a granddaughter of Itmad-ud-Daulah.

It is a gem of a building, set on a raised platform in a peaceful garden on the left bank of the Jumna, a tomb of perfect proportions with four octagonal minarets rising from the corners, a square cupola in the centre. Built wholly of white marble, it is covered with mosaics in the Italian *pietradura* style, with inlays of semi-precious stones of cornelian, agate, lapis lazuli, bloodstone and jasper all intricately worked into flowers and designs. Perhaps the most skilled example of craftsmanship lies in the incredible delicacy of the screens, each cut out of one block of marble, so finely carved they look like a tracery of lace.

There it basks in the sun, the marble screens filtering the slanting rays through to the interior, beautifully preserved for Indians and foreign tourists alike to see.

I wonder if this child from another age, standing on its steps, her face alight, knew the romantic story of Nur Jahan.

Princes

'The Raj' was born in 1858 when, as the embers of the Mutiny died away, the crown took over the government from the hands of the Honourable East India Company. The hereditary rulers of the independent princely states (amounting to one third of all India) were guaranteed their rights by the British who kept control of foreign affairs and only interfered internally to warn or depose a prince if they considered that gross misrule was taking place.

The states were governed by the same sovereigns as before in a feudal system. Within their pinnacled palaces the princes lived opulent lives, their large *zenanas* guarded by brawny eunuchs, their land defended by their own armies, their fortress homes sealed off by massive spiked gates to withstand the elephant cavalry of their enemies. Many princes were generous with their riches, bringing electricity and water to the people, building roads, reservoirs, schools and hospitals.

The maharajahs were each given a number of

C. Elgee.

gun salutes on their official visits to British India, twenty-one being the top number for the five highest-ranking princes. They were mostly pro-British—who else would give them a free hand to rule with power of life and death over their own subjects, they above the law themselves? The British in their turn were equally in favour of the princes, sharing a love of polo and *shikar*. An invitation to stay in one of the royal guest houses to enjoy tiger shoots, pig-sticking, hunting with tame cheetahs, and duck shoots from *jheels* where the wild birds flighted in their thousands, was prized indeed. Even royalty out from England was impressed by the lavishness of the entertainment, the well-organized sport, the hundreds of servants and the vast riches.

Then too as in the sketch there was the incredible pomp and circumstance of the yearly *Dussera* celebrations in the Hindu states. On the ninth and last day a procession moved through the city with bands, squadrons of cavalry and *chobdars* carrying elongated staffs of office. Most impressive of all was the maharajah, in a high-necked coat of cloth of gold, sitting in a golden howdah on a huge magnificently caparisoned elephant, making the *namaste* greeting constantly to this side and that as his people cheered themselves hoarse.

On the left of the picture showing the princes stands a *raj-kumar* (heir apparent), from his dress and red silk turban, of Jaipur. Beside him, wearing a jewelled flat cap, is one of the richest and most important of the princes, the Maharajah of Gwalior, descendant of the famous Scindhia of Gwalior, Prince of the Marathas, who successfully fought the Moghuls.

On the right, with the princelings, is the unmistakable figure of His Highness Fateh

Singh, the Maharana of Udaipur, who reigned until 1930. He lived in the high-walled and many-windowed City Palace looking across the peaceful Pichola Lake to his white marble Summer Palace, a cupola-roofed, domed, arched and balconied building. It had a hidden garden of splashing fountains where, in that *zenana* playground of purdah, the ladies pushed each other on golden swings, the whole fairy-tale palace seemingly floating between sky and limpid lake.

Of all the proud Rajputs whose red, yellow, blue and wine-coloured turbans—wound from up to thirty feet of thin *mulmul* (muslin)—vied in brilliance with the women's full skirts and mantles, the proudest was Fateh Singh, the Maharana. The only line of princes to bear that high title, the Maharana claimed descent from the god Rama from the foundation of his family in AD 144. The title continues to this day though the succession went through troubled times as the Residency Surgeon in Udaipur, who was a great friend of the Maharana, knew well (see page 72).

In the Durbar held in Delhi in 1911 for George V and Queen Mary, where their crowned Majesties draped in velvet trains sat in the open on a triumphal canopied podium to receive the homage of the princes in strict order of precedence, Fateh Singh of Udaipur was the most outstanding figure of that outstanding assembly. He was a very handsome elderly man, splendidly whiskered with a cleft white beard and proudly curling moustaches. His fine tall figure was clothed in intricately gold-spun satin robes over which he wore a necklace of diamonds and emeralds in sparkling strands, and a *pugri* studded with jewels.

Among the British officials watching from their reserved seats could be heard murmurs of disapproval when the Maharana came up to their Majesties and, giving them only a slight obeisance, turned and marched off straight-backed to his seat. The others, even His Exalted Highness the Nizam of Hyderabad, had backed away at least a few steps. But the Residency Surgeon of Udaipur smiled to himself as he watched his friend—it was not for the descendant of Sri Rama to bow abjectly before any man, even the greatest emperor in the world!

Nautch Girl

Singing and dancing girls were in great demand in India for festivals and at wedding parties where dancers before the chief guests in an upper room were accompanied by three or four instrumentalists, while, down below, in a crowded courtyard a lesser dancer, as in the sketch, twirled to the rival music of a tom-tom and zither.

Music was individually interpreted by each singer or musician who rendered his piece in his

own manner, yet all moved in a melodic whole. The strong beat with rhythm of quarter-tones perfectly accompanied the complicated techniques of the dancing girl. Every expression, every posture of her body, the movements of wrist and foot, her turn of head, gestures, gaits, and use of eyes (eyelids heavily painted in gold) were full of meaning. The hand gestures and her controlled footwork were particularly brilliant, and it was said she could sound separately each bell on her anklets. Dances told simple village love stories, and tales of war and heroic deeds. There were stylized temple dances and sensuous court dances, and the charming girl in the picture was dressed much as the fabled court dancer who brought such trouble to the maharanas of Udaipur.

A long time ago, the legend ran, the then Maharana became enamoured of a beautiful dancing girl who was also (as most were) an acrobat. He agreed to give her all the jewels and lands she wanted on one condition: that she would cross over a tightrope from his City Palace to his Lake Palace. She readily agreed. To her a tightrope was a tightrope and it really made no difference whether it was over land or water.

Late one day all was set for this daring act, the acrobat ready to start, the rope stretching from one palace to the other, sagging in the middle. The populace turned out in thousands to watch from the ramparts of the fortress, while the balconies and turrets of the City and Summer Palaces were crammed with courtiers and servants, the *zenana* ladies pressing their faces to the latticed windows the better to see the spectacle.

An exclusive party of males glided below in the red and green royal barge, many oarsmen wielding the dripping oars. On the high stern rose a tiered ornamental platform where the Maharana lay back on his silken cushions watching the alluring girl gracefully balancing her way towards him, a long pole in her hands, each dainty brown foot placed carefully and surely before the other, her silver anklets gleaming in the lowering sun, the little bells twinkling in the hushed silence.

The Maharana frowned as she progressed. He sat up as it dawned on him that she was going to reach her goal. She was already more than half way across! He would have to give her anything she asked—all those possessions! In a swift movement he drew his curving sword from its velvet scabbard and standing up to his full height he stepped forwards, and, with one lashing swipe, cut the rope. In the deafening quiet that followed, the cries for help from the dancing girl rent the evening air; those watching took their cue from the Maharana, none daring to move.

When she saw the barge turning away, the girl cursed. With her gasping, gulping, dying breath she cursed the despicable Maharana who had broken his word, and laid a curse on direct heirs succeeding for generations to come. The Pichola Lake waters turned crimson in the sunset as the lovely nautch girl sank for the last time, her spreading hair black and ominous upon the waters.

So it happened, though always there were found nephews or other relations to take the *Raj-Kumar's* place—and then Bhap-ji was born, growing into an intelligent, lively, handsome, sports-loving, healthy child. Yet he too became ill, very ill and near to death, the *hakims* in the palace unable to diagnose the sickness. Maharana Fateh Singh desperately called upon the Residency Surgeon, who looked after the political families and ran a hospital in the city.

In answer to the urgent message, the Residency Surgeon seized his black bag, mounted his buggy and trotted out up the road to the rambling City Palace. He was led through a maze of halls, corridors and passages to the sick boy, staying with him that night and for some days to come. He diagnosed infantile paralysis, and through his devoted care Bhap-ji's life was saved. In time he was able to shoot and play tennis standing at the net, though he was never able to walk without assistance, his slight figure humped and delicate.

Though no one voiced the thought aloud, it was in everyone's mind that even in the twentieth century the nautch girl's curse could strike.

On Fateh Singh's death Bhap-ji became HH The Maharana Sir Bhupal Singh Bahadur, GCSI, KCIE—but he never had a son and heir.

Nepalese

Nepal was virtually a closed country when this picture was painted thirty years before Everest was conquered. No foreigner without a special permit was allowed to enter the independent kingdom ruled by a hereditary maharajah prime minister and a king, the Maharaj-di-Raj, a godlike figurehead above affairs of state. The Raj was represented in the capital of Katmandu by an official with the imposing title of Envoy Extraordinary and Minister Plenipotentiary.

To reach this isolated country travellers went by rail to Raxaul in Bihar, from thence to the roadhead at Bhimpedi. After that it was shanks' pony, or hill *tats* as the sturdy little mountain ponies were called, for a two-day trek over the undulating lower Himalayas to the valley where Katmandu lies. There was a cableway running over the heights and spanning the gorges carrying small day-to-day essentials, but everything else was carried up on the backs of the Nepalese, many of whom were women as in the sketch at the top of the page.

With well-developed muscular calves, these short women were incredibly strong. They padded up and down the tracks on bare feet, helped only by a staff, bearing enormous loads of tea chests, kerosene, petrol, furniture, even pianos and people, the leather thongs across their foreheads leaving permanent indentations.

In that mountainous land of earthquakes and monsoon torrents, road works were daily in operation to keep the tracks open. Gangs of coolies, as in the lower sketch, carried away earth from minor landslides to places where the path had been eroded, two men always working together. Two men to one shovel—one man pushing, the other pulling with a string—was as usual a sight in Nepal as it was in India where it was said they had 'made an invention wherewith two men could do the job of one!'

In the war with Nepal of 1814 the British were so taken with the Tartar-featured, broad-chested, short-statured inhabitants that they began to recruit them into 'John Company's' army from the district around a village north of Katmandu called Gurkha, thus bringing into being one of the most loyal, bravest and toughest corps in the Indian Army. These Hindu men made brilliant fighters, terrifying the enemy with their short but lethal curved *kukris* with which they ritually decapitated goats and buffaloes during the *Dussera* festival. Their families were renowned for 'following the drum', the wives picturesque when in their national costumes with head-dresses of turquoise matrix and silver as in the picture.

I had a Nepalese ayah once. She was one of the jolliest people I have ever come across, her broad flat face with elongated eyes wreathed in smiles, and she was also an expert masseuse without ever having had a lesson, and a born knitter. She would make up a garment from just looking at a picture, knitting at incredible speed on long needles, one of which she kept tucked under an armpit. Intricate patterns resulted in exactly the right size without her apparently counting nor even looking at the stitches!

In the Simla Hills

Much has been written about the hill station of Simla, and much fun made of the goings-on there of the British women separated for months from their husbands who were sweating it out in the plains during the hot weather. The women enjoyed the cool air, smelt the sweet wild violets by mossy fern-strewn springs, and admired the green rhododendron bushes with their red blooms as they strolled along the Mall by corrugated-iron-roofed houses perched on hillsides and looking down on to the haze miles below. Much is known about those ladies but little about how the Paharis (hill people) lived, though there were some who ventured out beyond Chota (small) Simla on to the Hindustan–Tibet Highway.

The Paharis were physically taller than the Nepalese, more Mongolian of feature with high cheekbones and slanting eyes. They were both musical, playing their pipes as they walked the mountain paths, and superstitious—only planting out and harvesting their crops of rice, buckwheat and corn in their small terraced fields when the phase of the moon showed it was an auspicious moment.

The Pahari woman in the picture wears the old-style baggy Moghul breeches made of warm *puttoo* (home-spun wool), a nose-ring resting on her mouth, and carrying her youngest child in a shawl. The hair of the little girl beside her is braided with bright woollen threads. Other hill women from rugged Spiti higher up the Himalayan range could be distinguished on the road by their very long matted hair, which on closer inspection was not all their own but strands of yak's tail-hair, greased with rancid butter, woven in and plaited in thin strips to their knees. Yaks with their long hairy coats made strong beasts of burden as well as providing milk, butter and meat, the only oxen that could withstand the climate in the higher plateaux.

Fascinating encounters were made on this highway to Tibet, known as the H-T Road, the main artery to a vast mainly unmapped country. Like the Nepal road it was but a track hewn out from rock and hill, winding its way down valleys, across wooden bridges spanning gorges, and up precipitous sides to greater heights.

Rounding a corner there was a young man from Ladakh resting his pack of potatoes on a bank while he lit up his *chilum* stuffed with green tobacco. Pack trains were passed, the plaintive tone of the pipes and the ding-dong of the bells around the mules' throats carrying far across the valley. Herdsmen with their flocks of goats and sheep appeared, each sheep bearing its small burden of a pack of borax salt upon its back. There were ragged woodsmen by their blue-smoked fires, wine-red-clad Lamas from Tibet twirling their prayer-wheels, and *sahdus* with wooden begging bowls and their blackbuck skins, making their way to some cave-shrine where they would spend the summer fed by the nearest villagers.

There were the hill people and the sough of the wind and the smell of pine needles as soft to walk on as a thick-piled carpet, and the fresh odour of the deodars as the H-T highway passed through the forests where *langurs* chattered, the *bara-singh* rubbed his horns, and black bear roamed. And overhead a great lammergeyer flew, drifting with still wings on an upcurrent, eyes alert for prey, poised for an accelerating death-dealing stoop.

The Pearl of Hind

That was what the Moghul emperors called Kashmir. They also described it as an emerald set in pearls, a land they were so loath to leave that they sometimes left it too late and found themselves snowbound, a land they eulogized with words akin to those written on the frieze in the Hall of Audience at the King's Palace in the Red Fort, Delhi: 'If there be a Paradise upon Earth, it is this, it is this, it is this!'

There were two ways into this treasured Vale in the days before there was an airport. One went from Rawalpindi in the Punjab, following the tortuous path of the rushing Jhelum River to the rolling plain at over five thousand feet. The other way went from Jammu, the red and white stone winter capital of Kashmir where the Maharajah had his winter palace (Kashmir was one of the princely states with a twenty-one gun salute), the road twisting up the Pir Panjal range, and at the summit passing through the Banihal tunnel. Emerging, one was faced with a breathtaking view of the great wide valley lying some three thousand feet below. On either side towered range upon range of jagged ridges and great snow-clad mountains of far horizons to a beyond which no eye could fathom, the mind left free to soar with the mystics into infinity.

Whichever way one entered Kashmir, the freshness of the air at that altitude together with the beauty of the scene combined to make it an intoxicating experience. Before lay the Vale, indeed a jewel set in the white-capped pearls of the Himalayas, the fields the colour of emeralds with patches of ruby poppies, the lakes sparkling in the sun like diamonds of the purest water.

All was colourful here in early summer. The tall wooden farmhouses—in winter the lower parts crowded with livestock feeding on iris and willow leaves—were dark against the peach and almond trees blossoming in the hamlets. The flat earth roofs made natural gardens with striped scarlet and white tulips flowering amongst the grass. Tall sentinal poplars lined the straight roads; hobbled ponies browsed

on marshy land by water-hoists; old men stood bent double in the fields, and mothers with children came down to the lakes to draw water by willows whose delicate trailing fronds caressed the surface.

The women were dressed in maroon, brown or dark red waistless robes of heavy material, their headpieces of *pashmina*, the wool from the under-hair of the goat making so fine a material that it could be passed through a ring. Their sleeves were turned back by day, but when let down were long enough to cover fingers like a muff—useful in the frozen winters when the *banihal* (blizzard) blew. The men wore wide-cloaked *chogas*, beneath which in winter they hung from a strap round their necks a fire-pot wherein charcoal glowed red hot to warm and sometimes scorch.

The women of Kashmir are particularly fair-skinned, claiming—with most of the populace—to be descendants of Alexander the Great. They have huge liquid eyes and classical straight-nosed profiles, and used to wear their hair in thin plaits, long earrings like candelabra dangling, their arms jingling with silver bracelets. The grubby rosy-cheeked children were enchanting in their brightly embroidered skull-caps, the girls with a mass of tangled dark auburn hair—water-babies we called them.

In Srinagar, the summer capital, they lived in a jumble of rickety houses built of small red bricks, with tiers of carved wooden balconies jutting out crazily over the Jhelum beside shining pagoda-shaped mosques and temples. Thousands more lived on dove-grey shingle-roofed boats down the lesser waterways branching off from the Jhelum which bisected the city of Srinagar, seven picturesque wooden bridges on carved trestles spanning the river. Here in the bazaar and on the *Bund*, on houseboats and in stores, the carpet factories, fur shops, jewellers and silversmiths displayed the many fine arts of Kashmir. There was Suffering Moses with his carved walnut merchandise and papier-mâché goods depicting hoopoes and kingfishers; But-

terfly with his finely embroidered satin under-wear; Ken Hadow with his chain-stitched carpets and tapestries; Subharna the Worst, My Sainted Aunt, and the photographer Mahatta.

Beyond lay the Dal Lake from which the thousand-foot-high Takht-i-Suleiman (Throne of Solomon) with a Hindu temple atop rose almost directly out of the water. It was at its base in the Dal Kāt that the houseboats so popular with the British were anchored in winter, in summer being towed out further along the banks of the great expanse of water which lapped the shores of the famous Moghul gardens. For ship to shore transport *shikaras* as in the sketch were used, a kind of canopied taxi-gondola with curtains and patterned cushions as big as mattresses on which to recline. They were given names like Love-in-the-Mist, or Whoopee by their owners—humorous, cheerful, roguish-faced boatmen who paddled away in the stern and demanded exhorbitant fares from sahibs who were unaware of the going rate.

Autumn was a spectacular time to glide across to the Moghul *baghs* (gardens) in a *shikara*, over the clear waters of the Dal Lake full to the brim from the melting snows. On it grew great patches of water-lilies with leaves a foot across, the blooms known as Buddha's flowers, floating, not tied to earth by roots, the lotus—a symbol of life and spirit. The water-babies picked the buds and splashed hell-for-leather after the *shikaras* in their skiffs, bent on obtaining baksheesh.

The whole valley was ablaze with autumn tints, the lake giving a double radiance to the reflections of the mountains, the islands, the trees, so faithfully reproduced that one could scarcely tell which was true, which mirrored. The crab-apples and wild cherries, the hazel and walnut trees vied with each other in the brilliance of their yellows, golden-browns, reds and burnished coppers, while the majestic *chenar* trees, over three hundred years old, dominated all in the richness of their scarlet and gold mantles.

The Shalimar Bagh of 'Pale Hands I Loved' fame was secluded, tucked away from the Dal Lake by a canal, a peaceful garden of glorious views with gentle streams and fountains rilling through its slight decline. The Emperor Jahangir laid it out in a simple design which divided it into sections representing the eight parts of paradise. And for whom did he build this garden which he called paradise within a paradise? Who else but his Light of the World, his beloved Nur Jahan, the daughter of Itmad-ud-Daulah.

Much in India, as we knew it in the days of the Raj, has altered since these pictures were painted, but happily most of these characters in their colourful costumes can yet be seen in the villages, cities and palaces.

The lure and the magic are still there and with them those things that are without price, for the vast dry plains and the eternally snow-clad mountains have not changed—neither has the friendly welcome from its kindly warm-hearted people.